PRAISE ᵣᵤₙ

SOUL SURVIVOR

Soul Survivor is a brilliant guidebook for us all. It teaches us how to live through the tough times and to dignify the trials. It reminds us that every anointed ministry will bear the scars that can only come from living through the tough times. It is a gem of a book!

LYNDON BOWRING
EXECUTIVE CHAIRMAN, CARE

Mike Pilavachi has learned the hard way that the desert is the place where we meet Jesus. He writes with a passion for Christians to go into the desert places themselves and find the reality of God that is there. Refreshingly honest and personal stuff.

PETE BROADBENT
BISHOP OF WILLESDEN

Every time I hear Mike Pilavachi preach, he speaks my language. He makes me laugh, he makes me cry, and he uses every emotion in between to communicate the message of Christ to us all. In his new book *Soul Survivor*, Mike invites us to embrace the desert experience as a necessary part of our walk. After reading *Soul Survivor*, you will *run* to the desert.

RICK CUA
VICE PRESIDENT, CREATIVE
EMI CHRISTIAN MUSIC PUBLISHING

What draws people to Mike Pilavachi's message, and what I love most about him, is his transparency. Mike shares openly both the joys and the struggles of life, offering an honest look at the dry, dusty and barren places. But Mike doesn't lead us to curse the desert; rather, he urges us to find within it the beautiful face of God.

LOUIS GIGLIO

AUTHOR, *THE AIR I BREATHE* AND *WORSHIP AS A WAY OF LIFE*
DIRECTOR, PASSION CONFERENCES

I've known Mike Pilavachi since I was 11. I've also had the privilege of traveling the world with him for the last three years. One of the many things I love so much about Mike is that he tells it like it is. He is incredibly honest, and *Soul Survivor* is no exception. This book is not based on theory—it is about lessons learned through the ups and downs of life. I found *Soul Survivor* to be wonderfully refreshing. Ultimately, it's a book of hope and an encouragement and a lifeline to all who are seeking to live out their faith in the midst of a broken world.

TIM HUGHES

AUTHOR, *HERE I AM TO WORSHIP*
SONGWRITER AND WORSHIP LEADER

The more deeply we know the Lord, the easier it will be to "read His face" and sense what He desires us to do. Mike Pilavachi draws on his own experience and the Bible to infuse faith, hope and love in us and to inspire us on our journey.

J. JOHN

PHILO TRUST

In this book, firmly rooted in the soil of personal experience, Mike Pilavachi takes us on a wonderfully honest and deeply insightful journey into the desert—God's crucible for life.

MARTYN LAYZELL
WORSHIP PASTOR, SOUL SURVIVOR
WATFORD, UNITED KINGDOM

Though Jesus is the answer for everyone, Mike Pilavachi's story illustrates that Christianity isn't necessarily a life of quick and easy answers. Mike's honesty about his own human struggle will be an encouragement to anyone who is hanging on to God while walking through a desert experience.

ANDY PARK
AUTHOR, *TO KNOW YOU MORE*
WORSHIP LEADER

Mike's enthusiastic passion to encourage anyone and everyone who will listen to go further and deeper in their walk with God shines out from everything I have seen him do. His knack of achieving this in a straightforward and amusing way makes *Soul Survivor* essential reading for all those who have ever found themselves in a spiritual desert and are struggling to understand why. This book is honest without being self-pitying, and encouraging without being patronizing. Excellent stuff.

ANDY PIERCY
WORSHIP LEADER, HOLY TRINITY BROMPTON, LONDON
ALBUM PRODUCER FOR MATT REDMAN, DELIRIOUS?
AND GRAHAM KENDRICK

The theme of the desert is found constantly throughout the Scriptures, yet many of us have failed to grasp its significance for our lives. In this excellent book, my friend Mike Pilavachi takes us on a journey into the depths of the desert, unearthing important truths for our everyday walk with Christ. I grew up in Mike's youth group, and his teaching had a profound effect on my life. I pray his insights in *Soul Survivor* will have a profound effect on your life as well.

MATT REDMAN
AUTHOR, *THE UNQUENCHABLE WORSHIPPER*
EDITOR, HEARTOFWORSHIP.COM
WORSHIP LEADER

Soul Survivor ministered to me while in the midst of my own desert of sorts. It helped me to make sense of some of the difficult situations in my life and reminded me that the desert isn't a place of death but of deep and authentic life!

TOMMY WALKER
ARTIST AND SONGWRITER, INTEGRITY WORSHIP

Are you thirsty for God? Do you yearn to show the world how great God is but just don't feel prepared? Within the pages of *Soul Survivor* you will discover where you can find these longings satisfied. In one of those divine paradoxes, your greatest refreshment often comes during the driest of circumstances. *Soul Survivor* gives indispensable guidance from a fellow journeyer who can show you how to return from the desert deeper in love with your maker and empowered to make a difference in the world.

DARLENE ZSCHECH
AUTHOR, *EXTRAVAGANT WORSHIP* AND *SHOUT TO THE LORD*
SONGWRITER AND WORSHIP LEADER

SOUL SURVIVOR

MIKE PILAVACHI

Regal

From Gospel Light
Ventura, California, U.S.A.

PUBLISHED BY REGAL BOOKS
FROM GOSPEL LIGHT
VENTURA, CALIFORNIA, U.S.A.
PRINTED IN THE U.S.A.

Regal Books is a ministry of Gospel Light, a Christian publisher dedicated to serving the local church. We believe God's vision for Gospel Light is to provide church leaders with biblical, user-friendly materials that will help them evangelize, disciple and minister to children, youth and families.

It is our prayer that this Regal book will help you discover biblical truth for your own life and help you meet the needs of others. May God richly bless you.

For a free catalog of resources from Regal Books/Gospel Light, please call your Christian supplier or contact us at 1-800-4-GOSPEL or www.regalbooks.com.

Originally published by Kingsway Communications Ltd., Lottbridge Drove, Eastbourne BN23 6NT, England.

Original title: *Wasteland?: Encountering God in the Desert*

Cover and interior design by Robert Williams
Edited by KT Schuh

Library of Congress Cataloging-in-Publication Data

Pilavachi, Mike.
    Soul Survivor / Mike Pilavachi.
        p. cm.
Includes bibliographical references.
    1. Spiritual life—Christianity.   2.   Deserts—Religious aspects—Christianity. I. Title.
    BV4501.3.P55 2004
    248.4—dc22   2003017605

1 2 3 4 5 6 7 8 9 10 11 12 13 14 15 / 10 09 08 07 06 05 04

DEDICATION

To Tim Hughes, for your loyalty, forgiveness and partnership in ministry. To Pete Hughes—I so believe in you and look forward to all the crises we still have to share together. To Matt and Beth Redman, Maisey Ella and Noah Luca, my friends for life.

CONTENTS

FOREWORD

Mike Pilavachi is a remarkable and very lovable man. He is so honest and wonderfully open. I love his self-deprecating humor and his unpretentious attitude toward himself and his ministry. Thousands of young people hang on every word he speaks. They recognize that he is the genuine article because he lives it out and he speaks with great authority. Since he writes as he speaks, this book is not only immensely readable but also packed full of wisdom and valuable insights.

Nicky Gumbel
Holy Trinity Brompton
London, England

ACKNOWLEDGMENTS

I don't seem able to do anything without involving my friends, whether or not they want to be involved. So once again I am indebted to my long-suffering partners and friends in the ministry who have had to put up with my obsessive requests to "just read it again." I value you all more than I can say; and to do what I do without you would be unthinkable.

So thank you to Andy Arganda, Liz Biddulph, Catherine Berry, Tim Hughes, Pete Hughes, Martyn and Emily Layzell, Ali MacInness, Ken and Jeannie Morgan, Matt and Beth Redman, Rachel Shorey and Ruth Yule for reading the manuscript (often more than once!) and giving such honest and constructive feedback.

Thanks to Richard and Diana Scott and the extended Cole family for your hospitality and generosity. Thanks to Diana for helping to write the book, Richard for the chardonnay (or was it a cabernet?) and David for making me laugh. I do not refer here to your sense of humor.

From across the pond I would like to thank Bill Greig III for encouraging me to write this book in the first place. You are a gentleman. Thanks to my friends Alan and Rachael Siebenhaller for your encouraging and helpful comments.

Also my thanks go to all my friends in the Kingsway/Survivor family. To Les Moir and Malcolm du Plessis for your friendship and partnership, Dave Roberts, Richard Herkes and Carolyn Owen for putting it all together, and John Pac for your generous spirit.

Most of all, I want to thank the church I have the privilege to pastor, Soul Survivor Watford. You are an amazing bunch of people, and I know I don't deserve you. I love you very much.

CHAPTER 1

ENTERING THE DESERT

The urgent need for the Church today is not for more clever people to explain Jesus better. It is not for more attractive people who by their looks and personality will make Christianity suddenly more trendy and appealing. It is not even for more committed and disciplined people who will advance the cause of the kingdom of Jesus by grit and hard work. The great need today is for deep and authentic people.

British evangelist David Watson said something like this about 20 years ago. I believe it is truer today than it was then. In a superficial world that demands instant pleasures and then discards them just as quickly, the Church is in great danger. In our attempts to be culturally relevant we could, if we are not careful, become as shallow as the surrounding culture. That would be a great shame. These are days when growing numbers of people are becoming weary of hype, gimmicks and the quick sell. This generation is increasingly asking if there is something deeper than the slogan, something more lasting than this year's instant celebrity.

Jesus came to usher in another way. He called it the kingdom of God. More than that, He came to announce that He *is* the way, the truth and the life. He came to invite the world back to reality. He came to take us deeper. Many in the Church recognize that we are called to live in the real world in such a way that we make a difference. And so we must. We must engage with our neighbors and take a genuine interest in their lives. We have to listen to their stories and not just tell them our own. We must love them unconditionally. If any people have a mandate to care for this planet, it is surely Christian people, children of the creator. The Lord shouts from the Scriptures again and again that the agenda of caring for the poor, the marginalized and the hurt is the Christian agenda. He tells us that He hates, even despises, our religious feasts if we do not let justice roll down like a river and righteousness like a never-failing stream (see Amos 5:21-24).

Jesus came to invite the world back to reality.

Instead of engaging with the world, too often we act as if the church were a castle. We hide there together, protected by the moat, with the drawbridge up. Then once a year we feel guilty and decide to go out there and do some evangelism. So we spend a few weeks practicing our Christian dramas and Christian mimes and our testimonies. We are told never to go into enemy territory alone and so are sent out in pairs for safety. The day arrives, the drawbridge is lowered and we rush out to witness. After a week we run back to the castle of the church, dragging the few unfortunates we have captured more by accident than design. We raise the drawbridge and for the next few months do things to ensure that our captives cannot communicate with non-Christians either. And we call that evangelism. Antievangelism would probably be a more accurate description. The God who sent Jesus does not want us to let down the drawbridge and conduct hit-and-run raids once a year; He calls us to break down the walls of the church—to be a church without walls, a church for the community.

Two days before writing this, I took part in a youth festival. One of the other speakers told the young people not to forget the three legs of the Christian faith. She described these as prayer, Bible study and fellowship with other Christians. So far so good. She then told everyone to be very careful not to associate with nonbelievers. She advised the young people to have close friendships only with Christians. "Don't think you will lift a non-Christian up to your level," she said, "they will only drag you down to theirs." To illustrate the point she made a young man stand on a chair and try to pull her up. He couldn't. She then effortlessly pulled him off the chair and down to her level. As far as she was concerned, the case had been proved.

I am not sure it is possible to move much further away from the example of Jesus. He came to Earth and got His hands dirty. He ate with tax collectors and sinners. He befriended lepers and "sinful women." Why do we prefer to stay in the Christian ghetto where it is safe? I believe it is because we have a spirituality that just about works in church but does not work in the world. The bottom line is, we do not believe the Scripture that says, "The one who is in you is greater than the one who is in the world" (1 John 4:4).

TAKING A NECESSARY JOURNEY

Yet if we are to go further into the world and make a difference instead of being yet another voice that adds to the noise, we have to listen to the call to go on another journey—a journey into God Himself. If we are to offer life instead of platitudes, we need to catch more than a glimpse of glory. To attempt to change a world without being changed ourselves is a hopeless task. This is where the gospel of the Kingdom really is good news. Jesus Christ not only invites us to a new beginning, but He also offers us a new life and a new heart. He invites us on a journey that takes us to some unexpected places and, to be honest, some places that many Christians have been taught to avoid like the plague. Specifically, if we want to move in the power of the Spirit, to live the life of the Spirit and to carry a depth of spirituality that alone can change a world, He invites us on a journey into the desert. It is sometimes a very painful journey— a trip without the warm fuzzies—but it is, I believe, a necessary journey. This adventure is only for those who are committed to being a voice to, and not merely another echo of, society. It is for those who want to be passionately committed to Jesus, to the King and His kingdom. It is only for those who are sick of superficiality both in themselves and in the Church. Above all, it is for those who long to be "transformed into his likeness with ever-increasing glory" (2 Cor. 3:18).

Why have I written a book on how God uses the desert places to change us? So often it is in the desert that God prepares and shapes us for a life of effectiveness and power. The desert produces real people. The subject fascinates me. The fascination is not a detached, intellectual fascination but one that is deeply personal. I have spent a good part of my life in the desert. If I'm honest, I can't say I have enjoyed one minute of it. However, I am so glad for it. In the pain I have found purpose, in the suffering I have learned perseverance and in the loneliness I have met Jesus.

COMING TO THE END OF MYSELF

To start at the beginning, my parents emigrated from Cyprus five years before I was born. I was their first child and up until I started school I did not know any English children and spoke only Greek. My first day at school was a nightmare. When I realized that my mother was going to leave me on my own in this building with all these strange and loud human beings, I screamed the place down. The following months I remember as a time of complete isolation. Even when the language barrier improved, I remained painfully shy and spent the recesses walking in circles around the playground on my own while all the other kids played around me. I would count the seconds until

In the pain I have found purpose, in the suffering I have learned perseverance, and in the loneliness I have met Jesus.

the bell rang and my agony would be over until the next time. There were times when I used to hide behind a wall or in the bathroom until the bell rang so that no one could see me.

Although on the surface things improved over the next few years, a wound remained that has affected me ever since. All the way through my teenaged years I felt myself to be different. I was the outsider. Even when friendships came my way, I would expect them to break down, and often "what I dreaded . . . happened to me" (Job 3:25).

Then just before my sixteenth birthday, I met the Lord Jesus and became a Christian. At first the whole thing seemed so amazing. I had never needed much convincing that I was a sinner, but to discover such a Savior—that was almost too much to take in. To realize that God knew me completely and yet loved me, that He was committed to me and would never leave me nor forsake me (see Deut. 31:6) filled me with joy and hope. From the moment I met Jesus, I wanted to be a full-time pastor or missionary. But the opportunities did not come, and I had to concentrate on my studies instead. I was sure that once I had graduation under my belt God would launch me into a full-time revival ministry. To my surprise He didn't, and I found myself at Birmingham University for three years. After earning my degree, I took a "temporary" summer job in the accounts department of Harvey Nichols department store in Knightsbridge. They asked me if I wanted to sign a proper full-time contract so that I could take vacation and sick leave. I refused because I was convinced that within weeks I would be in Christian ministry. I worked for Harvey Nichols for eight years!

Those eight years were tough. I had sermons inside me but nobody would listen. Sometimes in my frustration I would preach to the mirror. Often the preaching was so anointed that I would go forward to recommit my life in response! I became involved in a local church and everything I tried seemed to go wrong. I ran an open youth club for unchurched young people, but it was closed down after the police had to intervene one night when we nearly had a riot. I organized an interchurch youth mission that hardly anyone attended. I even produced and directed a nativity play as an outreach to the community. It was a fiasco. One of the shepherds turned up drunk, and the angel Gabriel (who happened to be the church secretary) poured black coffee down his throat (to no effect) before his big scene. The inquest at the deacons' meeting afterward was one of the worst meetings of my life. While all this was going on, I found my job both stressful and boring. Accounting was not my gift, so I had to work twice as hard as everyone else just to keep up. (I still occasionally wake up in the morning in a cold sweat because my balance sheet won't balance.) I wondered if God had forgotten me.

As the years went on, I decided that the dreams I had would never materialize and that I would have to come to terms with life as it was. At first I struggled with feelings of bitterness and self-pity as I complained to God that life wasn't fair. There were times when the despair was overwhelming and the loneliness was almost unbearable. Then everything came to a head. I gave in to my feelings of isolation and began to withdraw from people. The dawning fear that I might never marry and have chil-

The desert is the place where God takes us in order to heal us.

dren ate away at me. Everything I had tried in ministry went wrong. Then division in the church leadership surfaced, and I found myself in the middle of the dispute. At the same time, some people whom I thought were close to me let me down. Eventually, I couldn't stand it anymore and ran away. I ran away from church and, for a short while, from fellowship. The worst part about the whole thing was that I could not run away from myself. Only someone who has suffered from depression can understand what it is like to look forward to bedtime every day and go to sleep hoping that in the morning the feelings will somehow go away.

COMING TO THE BEGINNING OF GOD

The desert is a dry place. Nobody goes to the desert in search of refreshment. The desert is an inhospitable place; it is not comfortable. The desert is an incredibly silent place; there are no background noises, no distractions to lessen the pain. The desert is the place where you have to come to terms with your humanity, with your weakness and fallibility. The desert is a lonely place; there are not usually many people there. Above all, the desert is God's place; it is the place where He takes us in order to heal us. I believe this theologically because I see the truth of it in the Scriptures. I also believe this experientially and personally as I have found it to be true in my own life. The worst of times can also be the best of times. While I was going through those eight "wasted" years, I would ask God regularly why He was taking so long to rescue me. Now my main question is, Why did He not keep me there longer? In that time my arrogance was dealt a mortal blow. My tendency to rely on my own resources and gifts was undermined so that I began to inquire of the Lord in a way I had never done before. My prayer moved from an attempt to persuade Him to bless what I was doing to a sincere searching to find out what He was doing and then spend my energy in blessing that. In the desert I saw my ambition for what it was and eventually came to the place where I determined to seek God for Himself, whether I had a ministry or not. More than anything else, I found that when I came to the end of myself, I came to the beginning of God.

"Where can I go from your Spirit? Where can I flee from your presence? If I go up to the heavens, you are there; *if I make my bed in the depths, you are there*" (Ps. 139:7-8, emphasis added). I discovered that God met me at my lowest point. He became my comfort. I knew His love for me when I felt myself to be the most unlovable. I developed a desperate hunger for His presence. For in His presence I began to be healed. Then in His perfect timing the desert came to an end. Doors that had remained shut for years suddenly flew open. I found myself in a land "flowing with milk and honey" (Exod. 3:17). I do not want to give the impression that since that time my life has been organized and I have gone from one spiritual victory to another—that would clearly not be true. I also do not want to suggest that I do not ever visit that place of pain. However, praise God, I do not *live* there any more.

There is an amazing verse at the end of the book of Song of Songs: "Who is this coming up from the desert leaning on her lover?" (8:5). There is purpose in the desert. The purpose is that we should return from the desert no longer leaning on our own understanding, strengths and talents but instead leaning on the Lord, whom we have discovered there to be our lover. In order to lean on Him, we must first acknowledge that we cannot walk by ourselves. Then we have to trust that the One we lean on will support us and hold us. Dependence and intimacy are the two major lessons we learn in the desert.

The journey to the desert and what happens in us and to us there is the subject of this book. Let's explore this dreadful and wonderful place together.

THE DESERT—GOD'S CRUCIBLE

There is a longing among many Christians today to know and move in the power of the Holy Spirit. We long to move in the same anointing that was demonstrated not only in Jesus but also in the Early Church. The first Christians didn't just talk about the gospel, they lived it. Listen to Paul:

> My message and my preaching were not with wise and persuasive words, but with a demonstration of the Spirit's power, so that your faith might not rest on men's wisdom, but on God's power (1 Cor. 2:4-5).

Many books have been written about spiritual warfare, many seminars attended on how we can heal the sick. In the Church there is a search for spiritual power. Jesus indeed promised that as His followers we would have power and authority in our proclamation of the Kingdom. How do we receive such power? The best place to start is with Jesus himself. In Luke 3:21-22 we read:

> When all the people were being baptized, Jesus was baptized too. And as he was praying, heaven was opened and the Holy Spirit descended on him in bodily form like a dove. And a voice came from heaven: "You are my Son, whom I love; with you I am well pleased."

What an amazing moment that must have been for Jesus. Indeed, every member of the Trinity got involved! Jesus was baptized in water, the Holy Spirit filled Him, and the Father spoke from heaven. To move in power we must be filled with the Holy Spirit. Jesus told the disciples in Acts 1:8, "But you will receive power when the Holy Spirit comes on you." Jesus was not only filled with the Holy Spirit, but He received the double whammy: His Father spoke to Him as well.

Anyone who knows me will tell you that I love being affirmed. I really enjoy it when people say nice things to me. If, for example, someone who reads this book were to write to me and say something like "Mike, your book was amazing—better than Shakespeare, better than Chaucer, even better than Jeffrey Archer. How did so much talent find itself in one human being?" I would be thrilled. It would make my month. Actually, it would make my year. I definitely prefer being affirmed instead of the opposite response: "Mike, I read your book. Is there any way I could have my money back?" If there is one thing, however, I prefer even to being affirmed, it is to be publicly affirmed. I love being publicly affirmed so much that if someone comes up and compliments me in a public place, I find myself saying, "Pardon? Could you repeat that a little louder? I am slightly deaf, so would you mind using the microphone?"

When Jesus was baptized in the river Jordan, He not only was filled with the Holy Spirit, but He was also publicly affirmed by His Father. The Father did not whisper, "Listen, Son, I love You and am pleased with You, but let's keep it a secret."

No, the Father shouted it from heaven! "You are My Son! I love You! I am pleased with You!" You might think that we need nothing more than an experience like this in order to move in the power of the Spirit. You would be wrong. Even for the Son of God this was not the end of the process. The very next thing that happens to Jesus after His baptism is both very surprising and very revealing.

The spiritual equation is this: Filled with the Spirit plus led by the Spirit into the desert equals returning in the power of the Spirit.

"Jesus, full of the Holy Spirit, returned from the Jordan and was led by the Spirit in the desert, where for forty days he was tempted by the devil" (Luke 4:1-2). What? No honeymoon? What went wrong? How can someone experience the filling of the Holy Spirit and immediately find himself in a desert? Surely the infilling of the Spirit is our passport to health, wealth and happiness.

Surely this is the beginning of the miracles and the ushering in of the Kingdom. Not for Jesus and not for us. Indeed, the Greek phrase translated as "led by the Spirit in the desert" can be associated with the words "driven by the Spirit." The same Spirit that filled Jesus drove Him into the desert. Why? We find the answer in Luke 4:14. After His encounter in the desert with the devil, "Jesus returned to Galilee in the power of the Spirit." The spiritual equation is this: Filled with the Spirit plus led by the Spirit into the desert equals returning in the power of the Spirit. We all love the filled with the Spirit part. Some of us love this so much that we are always seeking for more of the Spirit. Feeling low? Have another experience of the Spirit. Struggling to sense God's presence and hear His voice? Go to another receiving meeting.

I do not want you to misunderstand me here. Of course we need to be filled with the Spirit again and again. We should be hungry for more of God and that includes experiences of Him. After all, the Bible is full of people having encounters with and experiences of God. I believe, however, that at this point we can short-circuit a process that God has ordained for those He wants to use in His service. The process is a place. A spiritual place: the desert. When He has filled you, allow Him to lead you into the desert. Do not resist. When you find yourself in the desert place, don't be too eager to run back to the bright lights of the revival meeting. Stay in the desert and let Him teach you things you could never learn in any charismatic meeting. The desert is the place where God prepares you and forms you. It is His place. He waits for you there.

THE NECESSITY OF PREPARATION

Moses is a classic example of a human being who was prepared by God in the desert. A brief look at his story will shed some light on God's desert agenda for His people. Moses, though a Hebrew, was brought up in Pharaoh's household. While the rest of his people were slaves in Egypt, Moses had the best education Pharaoh could buy. Moses would have been brought up knowing how to hold his knife and fork. In other words, he was cultured. I have the impression that when the time came, Moses knew he was a cut above the other Hebrews. He thought he was God's gift to his people. He would be, but first God had to deal with him.

One day Moses saw an Egyptian beating up a Hebrew slave. Glancing this way and that, he killed the Egyptian and buried his body in the sand. "The next day [Moses] went out and saw two Hebrews fighting. He asked the one in the wrong, 'Why are you hitting your fellow Hebrew?' The man said, 'Who made you ruler and judge over us? Are you thinking of killing me as you killed the Egyptian?'" (Exod. 2:13-14).

Moses may have thought that his gifts, background and education qualified him to be ruler and judge over his people. He suddenly realized that his murder of the Egyptian had been witnessed. In one moment, he went from being a son of Pharaoh to living the life of a fugitive. He fled to the desert of Midian. There, one day, he came across a bush that was a little different from all the other bushes. God spoke to him from out of the burning bush and first revealed His character (see Exod. 3:1-6). He then commissioned Moses to go back to Egypt and lead the Hebrews out of their captivity. Moses' response is very interesting. He does not say, "At last! A job to suit my talents." Moses says, "Not me, Lord; send someone else. I'm not gifted enough. I'm not eloquent enough. The job's just too big" (see Exod. 4:10-13).

What has happened to Moses? He has lost his self-confidence. Maybe he needs therapy. The truth is that he has just had all the therapy he needs. He has had 40 years of therapy—that's how long he has been in the desert of Midian. It was in the desert that God did some surgery on Moses' heart. In the desert God took an arrogant, cocky young man and turned him into one of the most humble of men—in fact, the Bible describes him as the most humble person in all the earth (see Num. 12:3).

Numbers in the Bible have significance. Three is the number for God; six is the number for humans; seven is the number for completeness; eight is the number for new beginnings. I would like to suggest that whatever else "40" means, it means a long time. I'm sure Moses often felt it was too long. When we find ourselves in a spiritual desert, it nearly always seems too long. It actually never is. God's timing is perfect. He knows how long we need.

A day trip to the desert is quite a pleasant experience. We get out of our air-conditioned car and are stunned by the vastness, the dryness, the sand, the lack of water, the awesome silence. Then we get back into the car and drive away. Moses was not on a day trip. He was not there on a two-week package tour. He spent 40 years in the desert. It was dry, inhospitable and lonely. There are only so many sand castles you can build in 40 years! By the time he met the Lord at the burning bush, he was ready. He had been well and truly spiritually cooked. In the desert Moses came face-to-face with his spiritual poverty. He came to the place where he realized his gifts were not enough. A good education could not get him out of this hole. In the desert Moses met his weakness. Then he met God.

I love the way the Lord responded to Moses' statement of inadequacy. The Lord did not say, "Oh, come on, Moses. I've heard you speak; you're not that bad. Believe me, I've heard a lot worse. You're just having a crisis of confidence, that's all." At this point the Lord said to Moses all that he needed to hear. He said, "I will go with you" (see Exod. 3:12). The main lesson Moses learned in the desert was to trust in God and not in his own abilities and gifts. In the desert Moses came to the end of himself. In so doing, he came to the beginning of God.

In the Church we seem to prize gifting over character and skill over humble dependence. That is why we are so excited when someone vaguely famous becomes a Christian. We think God's purposes depend on us. In one sense they do, but only inasmuch as we depend on Him. After 40 years in the desert, Moses knew that God's work could only be done in God's way,

God's work can only be done in God's way, relying on God's power.

relying on God's power. It was a lesson he never forgot. In Exodus 33, in the midst of Israel's time in the desert, the Lord is so angry with His people that He tells Moses they can go into the Promised Land but it will be without Him. The implication is that the Lord will stay in the desert. Moses pleads with the Lord and He relents. Then Moses says,

> If your Presence does not go with us, do not send us up from here. How will anyone know that you are pleased with me and with your people unless you go with us? What else will distinguish me and your people from all the other people on the face of the earth? (Exod. 33:15-16).

Moses learned the secret. The secret is His presence. The thing that distinguishes us as Christians is not that we are better looking than everyone else. It is not that we are more intelligent, eloquent or talented. The thing that sets us apart is that we are the people of His presence. He has made us His dwelling place; His home is among us. He is called Immanuel, God with us. This is one of the great and vital lessons we learn in the desert. If we do not have Him, we have nothing. Apart from Him we can do nothing.

You could say Moses drew the short straw. He spent 40 years in the desert as preparation. Preparation for what? Preparation for 40 years in the desert with Israel! If there is any justice, then Moses' mansion in heaven will have a swimming pool, some fountains, multiple waterfalls—and it will be next to a lake.

THE LESSON OF HUMILITY

It is to Israel's time in the desert that we now turn. In Deuteronomy 8 we see two lessons that Israel needed to learn. The story is that Israel was coming to the end of her 40-year journey. As we see the people of Israel going around in circles in the desert (if they had walked in a straight line the journey should have taken 11 days), we realize that getting them out of Egypt was the easy part. In the desert God was working at getting Egypt out of them. In Egypt they had become used to being slaves. They had acquired a slave mentality. They learned to grumble and complain. They became used to having decisions made for them. They did not know how to take responsibility. And they learned the arrogance that comes to those who never have to be accountable for their decisions. In the desert God set to work on them.

> Remember how the LORD your God led you all the way in the
> desert these forty years, to humble you and to test you in order
> to know what was in your heart, whether or not you would

keep his commands. He humbled you, causing you to hunger and then feeding you with manna, which neither you nor your fathers had known, to teach you that man does not live on bread alone but on every word that comes from the mouth of the LORD (Deut. 8:2-3).

In the desert we learn humility so that we depend on every word that comes from the mouth of the Lord. The Hebrews made quite a mess of the desert. They complained about the lack of food. God then provided them with manna, and after a while, they complained about that. Moses went up the mountain to receive the commands of God, and while he was away, they built a golden calf and began to worship it. The list goes on.

They were His people whom He had called to be a light to the nations, so He had to humble them. *We* are His people whom He has called to be a light to the nations, and so He has to humble us. Humility is not the most enjoyable lesson to learn. In 1989 I was the youth worker at Saint Andrew's, Chorleywood. That year we began a conference for the family called New Wine. I was invited to lead the youth work. There were about 500 teenagers out of a total gathering of 2,500. We had a good week, but toward the end of the week something happened that was totally new to my experience—something amazing. People started asking me for an autograph. At first I thought they were joking. Then I began to enjoy it—really enjoy it. On the final morning two girls ran up to me and asked me to sign their Bibles. I did not have a pen and one of the girls lent me hers. I signed their Bibles with a flourish and added the regulation verse of Scripture. As they walked away I distinctly heard one girl say with joy to the other, "He touched my pen!" I was in ecstasy. It had finally happened. I had, at last, become a minor Christian celebrity! I walked around the campsite waving at everybody.

The last meeting of the conference was a communion service for all the family. I walked into the hall and wondered where I should sit. I decided that rather than sit with the other celebrities I would sit with the ordinary people. So I sat with Matt Redman's family. Next to me was Matt's sister Sarah who was about seven at the time. Then came the moment in the service where all went quiet as we contemplated the Cross. At that moment little Sarah turned to me and said in a voice that only a seven-year-old girl can muster, "Mike, have you always been fat or has it recently happened?" At first no one turned around, but after a few moments the whole row in front began to shake. Another few moments and people were pointing at me and laughing. I was humiliated. I wanted to die. I think I also wanted to kill Sarah. I left the room and complained to God. "How could You do that to me?" I asked. "How could You let that happen to a minor Christian celebrity?"

There is a verse that can be found in the book of Proverbs, in the letter of James and in Peter's first letter. It is quite simple. "God opposes the proud but gives grace to the humble" (see Prov. 3:34; Jas. 4:6; 1 Pet. 5:5). When God says something in the Bible, He means it. When God says something twice, He really means it. When God says something three times, then He really, really means it. He leads us all the way into and through the desert in order to humble us. God loves the humble. Proud people in the Kingdom are dangerous people. They eventually destroy more than they build. If we will not humble ourselves, then He will do it for us.

THE SECRET OF PRAISE

The second lesson of Deuteronomy 8 has to do with praise and thanksgiving. The children of Israel had been complaining nonstop about the conditions in the desert. They had been complaining about the manna and asking for something a little more interesting to eat. In this context the Lord says:

> When you have eaten and are satisfied, praise the LORD your God for the good land he has given you. Be careful that you do not forget the LORD your God, failing to observe his commands, his laws and his decrees that I am giving you this day. Otherwise, when you eat and are satisfied, when you build fine houses and settle down, and when your herds and flocks grow large and your silver and gold increase and all you have is multiplied, then your heart will become proud and you will forget the LORD your God, who brought you out of Egypt, out of the land of slavery (Deut. 8:10-14).

The Lord is saying here, "Learn to be grateful in the desert. Learn to thank Me for the manna when you wish it were steak. Learn to praise Me for the good land I have given you even though you have not entered it yet, and then when you do prosper you will not forget Me. If you learn the secret of praise and worship when life hurts, then when life is good you will not forget Me."

There is a peculiarly British disease that I have noticed infects virtually the whole population over the years. It is called grumbling about the weather. Most of the year when we meet, our conversation is laced with complaints. "What a horrible day; it's so gray." "I've forgotten what the sun looks like." "It's so cold—why can't we live in Spain?" Then one day the sun comes out and the temperature warms up. Do we rejoice? No. Instead we grumble even more. "It's very hot—it's all that global warming." "If it carries on like this, there'll be a drought and we will all die of skin cancer."

Sadly sometimes there is as much complaining inside the Church as outside. We may have been taken out of Egypt, but Egypt has not been taken out of us. Sometimes life may not be perfect, but God is good all the time. It is not that we should pretend that circumstances are not as they are, but either God is bigger than the circumstances or He is not. The question is, What do we actually believe about God? Do we believe He is bigger than the air we breathe? Do we believe He is Lord all the time or only when life seems to be going well? Praise in the desert is the response of faith to the revelation of His character and sovereignty. Praise is a choice. Anyone can praise and give thanks when they receive everything on their wish list. Only disciples still worship when it hurts. Praise in the desert releases the blessing of God. Paul wrote his letter to the Philippian church from prison and yet the letter is filled with rejoicing. He tells the Philippians at one point:

Only disciples still worship when it hurts.

> Do not be anxious about anything, but in everything, by prayer and petition, with thanksgiving, present your requests to God. And the peace of God, which transcends all understanding, will guard your hearts and your minds in Christ Jesus (Phil. 4:6-7).

Note the antidote to anxiety is prayer with thanksgiving.

I have a particular problem with mornings. I don't like them and they don't like me. We don't get along. Sometimes I have a suspicion that mornings came in with the fall of mankind. I struggle to believe they were part of the original creation. It has been said there are two kinds of Christians: those who wake up and say "Good morning, Lord!" and those who say "Good Lord, it's morning!" For much of my life I have been in the second category. Then a few years ago I heard someone teach on gratitude and thanksgiving. He said that he had learned a discipline that changed his life. Every morning he would give thanks for his life as soon as he woke up. He would then give thanks for every part of his body. He would pull off the bed covers and look at his feet. He then gave thanks for every toe. He then thanked the Lord for his ankles, his calves and so on. By the time he had finished, he was ready to face the day in an attitude of worship. I thought this was wonderful. I could not wait to begin to do this myself. I went to bed, set the alarm and was so excited it took me ages to get to sleep. Next morning the alarm clock went off and I awoke. "Good morning, Lord!" I exclaimed. I pulled off the covers and a terrible thing happened—I could not see my feet. For a moment, confusion and panic overwhelmed me. Then I had a brainwave. I thanked God for my stomach which He has fearfully and wonderfully made and which I had helped Him with!

The point is that we will all have seemingly many more reasons to grumble than to praise. This is especially true in the desert. Our God is encouraging us to go deeper into Him, to choose to trust Him when we don't understand and to learn to praise Him when it hurts. Either God works all things together for the good of those who love Him, who are called according to His purpose, or He doesn't (see Rom. 8:28). Praise is an act of faith. In the desert our little moans are magnified. Our grumbles and complaints scream through the awesome silence. In the desert, that which seems hidden is revealed. We cannot hide behind a mask of false spirituality there. Paul tells the Philippians that he has learned the secret of being content in any and every situation, whether well fed or hungry. That is why he keeps encouraging the Philippians to "rejoice in the Lord always. I will say it again: Rejoice!" (Phil. 4:4).

The lessons of the desert are for life. When we learn the secret of giving praise when we have nothing, we will not forget to praise when we have everything.

CHAPTER   3

FINDING MYSELF
IN THE DESERT

Do you realize how loud the world is? Our culture is full of competing
voices urging us to buy this or invest in that. If we only own this or have
a figure like that, then we will be OK. There are so many TV channels,
radio stations, newspapers, magazines, books and CDs that it is possible to go through a whole day without any quiet. Many of us do. We
wake up to the radio, watch TV over breakfast, listen to the walkman
on the way to work or school, are bombarded with information and
return to an evening of reality TV.

We have become so used to background noise that we don't notice it
anymore and we have no idea how much it affects us. Did you know that
many stores now play different types of background music in different
departments, because they think certain styles of music make us more
likely to buy certain products? So there is music that is more conducive
to buying clothes, music that makes us hungry and music to buy a bed to!

The background noise is not neutral in our lives. It helps to shape us.

TAKING AWAY THE NOISE

Many of us hide behind the noise of the world. If noise is keeping us company, we never have to be alone. For some people their greatest fear is being alone. They can't cope with themselves or they don't like themselves, so they hide. Some years ago a film was released called *Educating Rita* starring Julie Walters and Michael Caine. The basic plot was that of a working-class housewife from Liverpool named Rita who wanted to break out of her narrow life. She enrolled to study for an English degree at a university. Part of her "education" was meeting new people who taught her a more sophisticated way of life. She left her husband and moved in with another student, a girl who was the life and soul of the party. One day Rita came home and found her friend unconscious from a drug overdose. The next scene is in the hospital room as the girl comes around. Rita says in bewilderment, "Why did you do it? You had everything." The tragic reply was, "When the parties were over, the friends left, the music stopped, all I had left was me. That isn't enough. I can't live with just me."

When we can't cope with "just me," we hide from "me." Some of us do it with alcohol and drugs. Others do it through noise and relationships. They are all addictions. They are all emotional aspirins, taken to dull the pain. We think that if we just turn up the volume outside of ourselves it will drown out the cry of the inner voice.

God has another plan. He has a better idea. True Christianity is the opposite of escapism. You take drugs to run away; you receive Jesus to know the truth. The truth of Jesus sets us free. He takes us to the desert so that we can meet ourselves there. There is no background noise in the desert. All is quiet.

The desert is the place to discover God; it is also the place we discover ourselves. Many of us are like Rita's friend. The truth is, we don't like ourselves very much—so we avoid our own company. After all, why spend any more time than you have to with someone you are not fond of? Most of the driven people I have met are driven because they don't like themselves and they think that if they only manage to do something significant then they will *be* significant. If they only do something worthwhile with their life, then they will have self-worth. The problem with living like

Jesus knew who He was because He knew *whose* He was.

that is there is never any peace, never any rest. The good feeling that comes with each achievement only lasts a short time. Then you have to go again. Life becomes exhausting. It is like taking a perpetual exam that you know you can't pass.

Jesus knew a different way. He knew who He was. He had nothing to prove, so He never did things to win people's approval. He knew who He was, because He knew *whose* He was. The words at His baptism, "You are my Son, whom I love; with you I am well pleased" (Luke 3:22), were uttered before Jesus performed one miracle, before He preached any sermon and three years before He went to the Cross. He was secure in the love and affirmation of His Father. Jesus' ministry was not a frantic attempt to be somebody; rather, it came out of the security of knowing Himself as the beloved of the Father.

My friends Martyn and Emily Layzell were recently expecting their first child. Before the baby was born, Emily confided to me that she was worried she might not bond with the child. She expressed the fear of most would-be parents. "What if I don't love my baby?" Her labor was quite awful. It lasted seventeen hours before the doctors realized that she needed an emergency cesarean section. I visited Emily the day after Jack was born. The first thing I saw as I peered around the curtain in the hospital room was Emily holding little Jack (actually not so little Jack—he was nearly 10 pounds) and looking at him. I knew immediately that they had bonded. Emily told me she loved him from the first moment she saw him. I was tempted to say to Emily, "Why do you love him? He has given you nothing but pain. He gave you a backache for three months and then 17 hours of pain before being responsible for your having to be cut open! He hasn't done anything for you—he has never washed the dishes, bought you a Mother's Day card or changed his own diaper." However, there was no point. Emily could not help but love her boy.

We have caused God nothing but pain. We have given Him grief at every turn, and yet He loves us. We don't deserve it but that was never the issue—we just have to receive it. Those who think they are worthless find it difficult to receive the unconditional love of God. The Lord wants to quiet the inner voice that tells us we are worth nothing, so we may hear and receive the truth of His Word. The desert is one of the places God shows us His love. It is there He slows us down so that we are ready to receive it.

DISCOVERING WE ARE SICK

The painful truth is that when humanity turned from a relationship of dependence and trust in God, we lost more than relationship with God— we lost the only true means of knowing who we are. Speaking through the prophet Jeremiah, God said: "My people have committed two sins: They have forsaken me, the spring of living water, and have dug their own cisterns, broken cisterns that cannot hold water" (Jer. 2:13).

When we turn from the spring of living water, we try to satisfy ourselves by drinking from any contaminated pool. We then become contaminated and diseased. Instead of seeking healing, we live in denial that there is anything wrong. The desert is a place of healing. Before that, however, it has to be the place where we discover that we are sick. When all the props have been taken away, we come face-to-face with our bankruptcy. The gospel has to be bad news before it can be good news. In the desert we find that we are "wretched, pitiful, poor, blind and naked" (Rev. 3:17). Only then can we truly receive the Savior. Only when we truly thirst in the dry and arid desert can we begin to drink the living water.

How does this pan out in practice? I know that when life becomes hectic, and especially when it seems to be going well, I can settle for a satisfactory working relationship with the Lord. I go from meeting to meeting, event to event and begin to find self-worth and significance in what I do. I begin to live for the nice comments as the applause feeds me, and I start to crave more. The trouble is, as with any drug, it is never enough. Then, because He loves me, the Lord gets to work: someone writes me a nasty letter; there is a misunderstanding in a relationship; a meeting goes badly; worst of all, no one laughs at my jokes. *What is the point of doing all this,* I ask myself, *when they don't appreciate me?* I then enjoy a good dose of "pity me." My craving for recognition and applause is suddenly not satisfied—my supply has been temporarily cut off. I am faced with a choice. Either I can find a shovel and frantically dig a broken cistern that will briefly bring respite, or I can sit in the desert and face my pitiful poverty. I can choose to face reality—the poverty of my motives, the nakedness of my ambition, the blindness of my heart. This is painful. That is why we avoid it.

We have a tendency to do anything and everything we can to avoid pain. We see pain as an enemy and will go to great lengths in order to live pain-free lives. Pain is actually a friend. Pain is a God-given way of telling us something is wrong. Imagine if your appendix burst and you did not feel any pain. Very soon you would be dead. The same applies to emotional pain. Instead of taking an emotional aspirin or denying that there is a problem, we must ask God and ourselves what the pain is telling us. Then we need to ask how we can deal with the cause of the pain and not simply relieve the symptoms. We need to stop living in denial and face the truth, because only the truth sets us free.

WAITING FOR HEALING

What is the alternative to finding the temporary relief that all broken cisterns provide? It is to wait in the desert when we find ourselves there. This is not at first glance an attractive option. It is, however, the only option for those who want to pursue God and who know lasting freedom is only found in Him. (Only when we discover who we belong to can we answer the age-old question, Who am I?) God is not into relieving the symptoms. He is into healing the cause. Did your mom ever tell you "All good things come to those who wait"? Mine did. I never did listen to her. I have since discovered the saying to be true if I want change, not just temporarily and on the outside, but permanently and within. The time in the desert always seems too long. Then, when we think we can't bear it anymore, He walks across the sand to meet us. He comes to bind up the brokenhearted, to set the captive free. When I look inside and face my own poverty, the goodness of His grace is good news—it is the gospel.

We know that drug and alcohol dependence are often attempts to escape reality. The truth is, all other forms of dependence are seeking to do the same thing. We can be people dependent, success dependent, even chocolate dependent. They are all attempts to escape from the desert. Don't escape. Don't run away. Don't drink anymore from a broken cistern. Let the desert make you really thirsty; then cry out for Jesus, the living water. Accept no imitations.

C H A P T E R 4

FINDING GOD IN THE DESERT

Of all the lessons God has for us in the desert, and there are many, the most important and the most wonderful is not so much a lesson as an encounter. In His mercy, God leads us into the desert that He may meet us there. He wants to capture our full attention. He wants to capture our hearts. In the desert there are no distractions, no competing voices.

There is a sense in which the title of this chapter is slightly misleading. God finds us before we find Him. Did the returning prodigal son find his father, or did the father find him?

One of my favorite verses in the whole Bible comes from the book of Hosea. Israel has turned from her God (her husband, to use the language of Hosea) and has allowed herself to be seduced by every passing idol. The Lord speaks of His anger and His pain. Then in chapter 2, verse 14, we read the most amazing words: "Therefore I am now going to allure her; I will lead her into the desert and speak tenderly to her."

What should a thoughtful and wise young man do to allure a lady? May I offer a little advice? First, he should put on clean socks. Then he should invite her out for a meal and tell her to choose anything her little heart desires from the menu. Most important, he should spend the entire evening asking her questions about herself and listening in rapt attention as though hanging on her every word. Then he should walk her home and soon after call to thank her for a wonderful evening. Of course, he doesn't need to worry about all that rubbish once he has married her, but that is definitely the way to allure her. (I think I may receive one or two negative letters as a result of this paragraph!)

How was the Lord to allure Israel, to restore her to her first love? He would lead her into the desert and there speak tenderly to her. It is not that He had never spoken tenderly before. The truth is, there were so many distractions around that she could not or would not listen. In the desert all the other voices are stilled. In the desert we listen.

The greatest national disaster for Israel in the entire Old Testament was the exile to Babylon. They were removed from the land that God had promised them, the Temple of Solomon was destroyed, and pagans ruled them. Israel's major story was their exodus from exile and slavery in Egypt and their journey to the Promised Land. Exile from this land was a disgrace and humiliation, and above all, a sign that God had abandoned them. The exile was Israel's desert. The national disaster of the trip to Babylon was more than a punishment for Israel's rebellion, it was also God's means of grace and mercy. Israel was shaken out of her complacency. In Babylon she began to listen again to the voice of her husband, her God, as He spoke tenderly to her: "By the rivers of Babylon we sat and wept when we remembered Zion" (Ps. 137:1). The Lord seems to speak the most tenderly in the darkest places; His comfort is the sweetest in the most painful times. The Song of Songs wonderfully illustrates this. This Old Testament book is essentially a love story between a king and a maiden, the "lover" and the "beloved."

A DESIRE FOR GOD

When I first became a Christian at age 15, I decided to read the Bible from Genesis to Revelation. Genesis was fine, Exodus interesting, the next three books rather difficult, but the story became more interesting again with Joshua and Judges. Eventually I finished Ecclesiastes, and then, after taking some antidepressants, I turned the page. The title of the next book, "Song of Songs," did not give any indication of what was in store. I thought it was a book about singing worship songs. After the first few verses, I was wide-eyed. I thought, *Who put this in the book? I don't believe it—someone's spiked my Bible!* The book is a passionate love story between a king and his maiden. Here is a short excerpt of the beloved speaking: "Like an apple tree among the trees of the forest is my lover among the young men. I delight to sit in his shade, and his fruit is sweet to my taste" (Song of Songs 2:3).

Imagine a girl talking like that today about her boyfriend. Descriptions have changed, although the sentiments, I think, have stayed the same! Later on in the chapter we read a wonderful, poetic passage:

Listen! My lover! Look! Here he comes, leaping across the mountains, bounding over the hills. My lover is like a gazelle or a young stag. Look! There he stands behind our wall, gazing through the windows, peering through the lattice. My lover spoke and said to me, "Arise, my darling, my beautiful one, and come with me" (Song of Songs 2:8-10).

The picture this conjures up is one of the lover coaxing the beloved out of her house and the two of them running together across the fields. If this were a Hollywood movie, the credits would appear at this point.

The perfect ending again. The Bible, however, is much more true to life than Hollywood ever could be. The first four verses in Song of Songs chapter 3 follow this scene. They are among my favorites in all the Scriptures.

For those who have never known themselves as the beloved, His presence is not missed.

All night long on my bed I looked for the one my heart loves; I looked for him but did not find him. I will get up now and go about the city, through its streets and squares; I will search for the one my heart loves. So I looked for him but did not find him. The watchmen found me as they made their rounds in the city. "Have you seen the one my heart loves?" Scarcely had I passed them when I found the one my heart loves. I held him and would not let him go till I had brought him to my mother's house, to the room of the one who conceived me.

The very next scene after the romantic climax is of the beloved tossing and turning in bed because her lover has disappeared. She has a choice at this point. She can either take a sleeping pill and go to sleep, or she can forgo her comfort, get out of bed and walk the deserted streets in the middle of the night, searching until she finds him.

There are times when the Lord, our lover, withdraws the sense of His presence to stir up in us a greater desire for Him. Will we get out of our spiritual beds, leave our comforts behind and search for Him? Will we seek after Him until we find Him? When we find Him, will we hold Him and *never* let Him go until we have allowed Him into the core of who we are? When the beloved brought the king "to the room of the one who conceived me," it was to the most intimate of places. The Lord sometimes hides His face, not to play Hide-and-Seek with us, but to allure us. There is a saying, "Absence makes the heart grow fonder." Sadly, for some Christians, for those who have never known themselves as the beloved, His presence is not missed. It is business as usual. I heard someone ask once, "If the Holy Spirit left your church, would anybody notice?" The desert separates the spiritual men from the boys. Will we walk the streets until we find the Lord in a deeper way? Will we choose to sit in the desert until we hear Him speaking tenderly to us? Or will we take the easy option and settle for

Search for Him until He finds you.

less than the best? God is not interested in a satisfactory working relationship with His people. The passionate God wants a love affair with His Church, a love so strong that we know we could never live without Him. The desert is God's means of taking us to that place of greater desire.

Biblical Christianity is so much more than an intellectual exercise. Some are afraid of emotions in the Christian life, because they recognize the danger of our faith becoming subjective and feeling centered as opposed to God centered. Yet the idea that our minds are objective but our emotions subjective is ridiculous. Of course, our relationship with God must progress from emotion to action, from feelings to obedience. Our faith needs to develop from intellectual assent to obedience. However, our emotions are part of our humanity. The appropriate response to God's revelation of Himself is intellectual, emotional and volitional. In this context I want to affirm that the Bible invites us to a relationship with God that is intimate. Intimacy does not have to mean sloppy sentimentalism. It does, however, involve a love that is of the heart as well as of the mind and will. Indeed, when God captures our hearts, our minds and wills (and wallets) follow. I encourage you to allow yourself to fall in love with the Almighty. You can have intimacy with His majesty! Search for Him until He finds you. Do not be satisfied anymore with a satisfactory working relationship. When you discover Him as the answer to your deepest longings, you will hold Him and never let Him go.

THE HEARTBEAT OF GOD

The apostle John has always fascinated me. He and his brother James were nicknamed sons of thunder, not because they were good at forecasting the weather, but probably because they had short fuses. So many of us have given ourselves labels or have had them given to us. I wonder what effect John's label had on him. Toward the end of his Gospel, John describes himself as "the disciple whom Jesus loved" and "the beloved disciple" (John 21:7,20). He wrote some of the most beautiful words on the love of God in the whole New Testament: "Dear friends, let us love one another, for love comes from God. Everyone who loves has been born of God and knows God. Whoever does not love does not know God, because God is love" (1 John 4:7-8).

What changed John so that his description would change from son of thunder to the beloved disciple? Spending three years with Jesus is the obvious answer. If there was one incident, however, that transformed him more than any other, it was probably the Last Supper as recounted in John 13. John is described as the disciple who was leaning on Jesus' chest. As he did so, he literally felt the heartbeat of God, beating with love for him. John was changed, not simply because he knew truth about Jesus (although that is important), but also because he encountered Jesus *as* the truth. To come to such a place of intimacy that we sense the heartbeat of God is to be transformed. In the desert, when all distractions are taken away, we are able to sense His heart beating for us and for a broken world.

After little Jack Layzell was born, his father, Martyn, would hold him and gently tap rhythmically on his back. Jack would promptly go to sleep. I noticed this and asked Martyn what he was doing. "Jack is used to his mother's heartbeat; as I tap the same rhythm on his back, he feels safe and falls asleep." In the desert our Father speaks tenderly to us. He shows us His love. It is there we change as we feel His heart beating for us. We assume a new identity. Instead of labeling ourselves "son of failure" or "daughter of anorexia," we begin to know ourselves as the disciples Jesus loves.

CHAPTER 5

A VOICE, NOT AN ECHO

Into a world of the sound bite and the sales pitch, a world in which words have no value beyond the day they are spoken, Jesus, the eternal Word of God, spoke—and His words will last forever. Don't you find it interesting that the gossip that is so fascinating to the media today is completely forgotten tomorrow, and yet the words of Jesus, uttered two thousand years ago, are still being quoted even by those who would never describe themselves as His followers? The reason is obvious. Jesus had something to say. He spoke with authority and conviction. Even His enemies recognized that.

God's desire is that His Church speak with the same authority and conviction so that people may say it is disturbing or provocative, even subversive, but at least no longer boring. Too often our message has seemed so irrelevant to the needs and cares of the world. Instead of being a prophetic people speaking to the culture in a language they understand about values that are eternal, we have all too often retreated into our own language code that is incomprehensible to the outside world.

LISTENING TO GOD'S VOICE

Two thousand years ago God sent a man to prepare Israel for the coming of Jesus. This man was a prophet. When he spoke, people knew he had something to say. His name was John the Baptist.

> In those days John the Baptist came, preaching in the Desert of Judea and saying, "Repent, for the kingdom of heaven is near." This is he who was spoken of through the prophet Isaiah: "A voice of one calling in the desert, 'Prepare the way for the Lord, make straight paths for him'" (Matt. 3:1-3).

No one is sure what John was doing in the desert or how long he had been there. One theory is that his parents, who were both quite old when he was born, died when he was a boy, and the Essenes, who lived in the desert, adopted him and brought him up there. Whether or not this is true, it is very interesting that the first description of John the Baptist is of "a voice of one calling in the desert." People recognize when someone has something to say and they flock to listen. This was true of Mother Teresa of Calcutta. A little Albanian nun who spent most of her life with the poor and the dying in one Indian city was welcomed and listened to by prime ministers and presidents around the world.

Nelson Mandela was an old man who had held no office or position of power when he was finally released after spending 27 years in prison. Yet upon his release he held no bitterness but instead a desire to forgive and build a rainbow nation. This attitude resulted in his becoming a voice that carried great moral authority. Mandela became the first democratically elected president of South Africa and held that office from 1994 to 1999. Today, this quiet and unassuming man, who lives simply, is still regarded as one of the most influential people alive.

So it was with John the Baptist: "People went out to him from Jerusalem and all Judea and the whole region of the Jordan" (Matt. 3:5). People didn't flock to a convention center to hear him; they did not switch on the TV to watch his show—they went to the desert. They went in the searing heat and sacrificed their comfort in order to hear what he had to say. Why? I believe it is because John the Baptist was a voice, not an echo. Whatever took him to the desert, while he was there the Lord made him a voice. God prepared John in the wilderness so that he in turn could "prepare the way for the Lord." So often we are echoes, repeating what we have been told with little conviction and no authority. Worse, we are mere echoes of the culture around us. We take on its values and dress them up in nice Christian clothes. We use the same marketing techniques, play the same games and then wonder why we are not taken seriously. An echo is a faint copy of the real thing. Too often we are a faint copy of the world.

RECEIVING OUR OWN VOICE

We find our voice when we find God in the desert. There He speaks tenderly to us. How desperate are we to hear His voice? Many church leaders go to conferences on church-growth principles and hear how if they follow certain strategies their church will grow. There are so many quick-fix solutions around for the problem of a dying church: If only we transition into a cell church; no, that won't do anymore—it has to be the G12 model. If we just engage in spiritual warfare over the principality governing our area, then revival will be released. If we only go to Toronto, Pensacola, Bogotá, Timbuktu . . . I am not against any of these things or any of these places, but surely we are missing something vital—*have we heard the voice of God?* Jesus said He did only what He saw the Father doing; He spoke only the words that the Father gave Him to speak. There was a cost for Jesus to hear the Father's voice. Often He prayed through the night on His own or went to lonely places to listen to His Father. We cannot rush these things. The quiet place, the lonely place, the desert place is never an easy place, but it is the best place because it is where God speaks to us.

How desperate are we to hear His voice?

One day Jesus took Peter, James and John to what has become known as the Mount of Transfiguration to have a prayer meeting. While Jesus was praying, His whole appearance changed and He began to radiate light. Then Moses and Elijah appeared and had a brief conversation with Him. The scene must have been awesome: Jesus was revealed for a moment in glory and two of the great heroes of Israel's history were seen talking to Him. How would you have responded if you had been present? Would you have cried out in excitement? Would you have fallen on your face in reverence and awe? Would you have stood there, speechless? This is how Peter responded:

As the men were leaving Jesus, Peter said to him, "Master, it is good for us to be here. Let us put up three shelters—one for you, one for Moses and one for Elijah." (He did not know what he was saying.) (Luke 9:33).

Can you believe it? At a time like that Peter wanted to begin a building project! As a response to the revelation of glory this left something to be desired. I have the impression Luke thought so too. That is why he felt it necessary to add in parentheses: "He did not know what he was saying." The response from heaven is wonderful and reveals the main purpose of the transfiguration of Jesus.

While he [Peter] was speaking, a cloud appeared and enveloped them, and they were afraid as they entered the cloud. A voice came from the cloud, saying, "This is my Son, whom I have chosen; listen to him" (Luke 9:34-35).

In sending the cloud while Peter was still speaking, God was essentially saying to Peter, "Shut up." Then He let Peter know that the appropriate response was to listen.

Poor Peter, he would have been at home among modern Christians. Whenever there is a fresh revelation of the glory of God, we usually respond by trying to build something. As with Peter, our Father longs for us to stop our activity for a while and listen to His Son. When we hear His voice, we have direction, we have confidence, we have authority—in other words, we have a voice! Don't just do something—stand there. Wait for as long as it takes until He speaks to you. Only then will you have something worth saying. It is not just that He speaks to our minds in the desert, but He also deals with our souls so that we have something authentic and therefore unique to say. Who we have become speaks as powerfully as what we say.

> John's clothes were made of camel's hair, and he had a leather belt around his waist. His food was locusts and wild honey. People went out to him from Jerusalem and all Judea and the whole region of the Jordan. Confessing their sins, they were baptized by him in the Jordan River. But when he saw many of the Pharisees and Sadducees coming to where he was baptizing, he said to them: "You brood of vipers! Who warned you to flee from the coming wrath? Produce fruit in keeping with repentance. And do not think you can say to yourselves, 'We have Abraham as our father.' I tell you that out of these stones God can raise up children for Abraham. The ax is already at the root of the trees, and every tree that does not produce good fruit will be cut down and thrown into the fire. I baptize you with water for repentance. But after me will come one who is more powerful than I, whose sandals I am not fit to carry. He will baptize you with the Holy Spirit and with fire" (Matt. 3:4-11).

When you encounter God in the desert and as a consequence become a voice to your neighbors, certain things happen to you. John did not care what people thought of him. He was not a slave to the latest fashion trends; he didn't have to be seen in the best restaurants! But seriously, when he saw the Pharisees and Sadducees coming out to him, he immediately had discernment as to who they were and what was in their hearts. I have noticed that those who spend the most time alone with God are also usually the ones who understand people the best. John knew, but he didn't just know—he acted on that knowledge. The Pharisees and the Sadducees were pretty influential in Israel. It was a brave man who crossed one of them but to offend both was to play with fire. John knew who he was and he knew his mission. When you are a voice, you shape events—they no longer shape you. When you are a voice, you persuade people—they no longer persuade you.

Most important, John the Baptist was a voice because he knew what his purpose was and what it wasn't. He knew the limits of his calling. He said, "Someone's coming who is more powerful than me, who is more important than me."

In John's Gospel, John the Baptist is quoted as saying, "He must become greater; I must become less" (John 3:30). John came to prepare the way for Jesus, and when the time came, he knew how to fade into the background and allow Jesus to take center stage. We, too, are called to prepare the way of the Lord, to proclaim His coming, to witness to His love. We must never forget that He is the star of the show; we are only the supporting cast. Our call-

When we hear His voice we have direction, we have confidence, we have authority—in other words, we have a voice!

ing is to make Him famous. Until we are dealt with in the desert, we want to be the star; we crave center stage. We don't know our purpose in life, so we are always trying to find one. The saddest people are those who don't know who they are or what they are here for. They spend their life striving to succeed, to be famous and to make lots of money, but they are never satisfied, never at peace. They see every mountain climbed simply as a launching pad for the next one. They are always traveling but never arrive. The desert kills this superficial existence in us and replaces it with depth. We discover from God our identity and purpose. John knew he was a voice. He knew what he was on Earth for— to prepare the way of the Lord. He was the friend of the Bridegroom. He rejoiced in the appearance of Jesus, and then, knowing his job was done, he stood to the side and joined in the applause.

My friend Matt Redman often tells a story about a donkey. There was once a donkey who came rushing up to its mother one day and said, "Mom, you won't believe what happened to me today. I was standing on my own, tied to a post, when two men came and untied me. They then led me down the middle of this road. You won't believe this, Mom, but lots of people came out of their houses and started waving at and cheering for me. Some even tore branches from the trees and waved them at me. Then some of the men took off their coats and laid them in the middle of the road, so I could walk on them. They did it for me, Mom. I must be famous!" The mommy donkey looked at her little boy and said, "Oh, my son. When they clapped and cheered and waved and laid their coats on the ground, it wasn't for you—it was for the one who was riding you."

Matt then says, "Whenever I lead worship and people start cheering and clapping and singing 'Hosanna,' I think of that Palm Sunday donkey and remember that they are not cheering for me. The applause is for the One who is riding on our praises. I remember I am just the donkey."

C H A P T E R   6

THE MOUNTAINTOP AND THE VALLEY

I became a Christian when I was 15. Meeting Jesus literally changed my life. The aspect of becoming a Christian that affected me most was the knowledge that my sins were forgiven. I could hardly believe it, and yet it was true. I did not need much convincing that I was a sinner; to find that there was an answer to my problem was good news. The main stumbling block to Christianity for some is the problem of sin. They are offended that they should be branded with the label "sinner." They say, "We have our faults, our little ways, but at heart we are decent, good people."

How easily we deceive ourselves. The word "sin" is just not politically correct today. It's an old-fashioned word. We prefer other nicer phrases. For me, one such phrase is "what I do when I'm tired." This is not a description so much as an excuse. So when I am impatient with someone, rude or downright selfish, it is not my fault, that's just what happens when I am tired. My favorite substitute phrase, however, is "my little weakness." This can sound almost cute. "My little weakness" could be "my little chihuahua." Jesus did not die for "what I do when I'm tired," nor did He die for "my little weakness"; He died for my sin. I feel sorry for those who don't think they have sinned very much because they can never understand how much they have been forgiven.

I knew I was forgiven, and it was wonderful. The forgiveness that comes from the cross of Jesus is the foundation of our faith. It may be a stumbling block to some, but it is the glory of the gospel. A few months after I met Jesus, I discovered that He not only forgives my sin, but He also wants to fill me with His Holy Spirit. I prayed to be filled with the Holy Spirit, and it was a glorious experience. I was on the mountaintop for weeks. I knew that He was with me and loved me, not only because the Bible told me so, but also because now I felt His love as an experience. The feeling is still hard to describe. Someone once said it is like "waves and waves of liquid love sweeping through me."

There are many descriptions in the Old Testament of times when the Lord manifests His glory among His people. One classic example is the time the people of Israel dedicated the Temple they had just built to the Lord:

> When Solomon finished praying, fire came down from heaven and consumed the burnt offering and the sacrifices, and the glory of the LORD filled the temple. The priests could not enter the temple of the LORD because the glory of the LORD filled it. When all the Israelites saw the fire coming down and the glory of the LORD above the temple, they knelt on the pavement with their faces to the ground, and they worshiped,

and gave thanks to the LORD, saying, "He is good; his love endures forever" (2 Chron. 7:1-3).

The "glory of the Lord" here is not merely a theological truth, it is an overwhelming experience. The priests could not enter the Temple. The people knelt with their faces to the ground.

Some struggle with the whole concept of experiencing God. They fear that to emphasize experience and feelings as legitimate ways of knowing God somehow detracts from the authority and uniqueness of the Bible as the place where God reveals Himself and His ways. I cannot see this. The Bible itself tells of the experiences people had of their God. Take all the experiences out of the Bible and you are left with a much smaller book. The Bible teaches that we can know God and love Him with all our minds and with all our hearts. The question we should be asking is, Are the experiences biblical?

I am an evangelical. I believe the Bible is the supreme and authoritative way that God has chosen to reveal Himself. We can trust this Book, and therefore we can believe the experiences of which it speaks. There is a saying:

The Word without the Spirit, you dry up;
The Spirit without the Word, you blow up;
The Spirit and the Word, you grow up.

The Bible and the Holy Spirit are not rivals; to honor both is to live a balanced Christian life.

Among Jesus' final words to the disciples before His ascension were these: "But you will receive power when the Holy Spirit comes on you; and you will be my witnesses in Jerusalem, and in all Judea and

Samaria, and to the ends of the earth" (Acts 1:8). Then on the Day of Pentecost the Holy Spirit came upon them with such power that many thought they were drunk.

There are great views from the top of the mountain— it is the place where we receive fresh vision.

There have been many times when I have felt God since that first time He filled me with His Spirit. There have been conferences and festivals where His presence was so tangible that nobody wanted to leave the meeting. These are mountaintop experiences. I believe such experiences are good and are part of God's provision for His people. There are great views from the top of the mountain—it is the place where we receive fresh vision. It is exciting up there; the wind of the Spirit is bracing and invigorating. I have come to believe, however, that God does an even deeper work in us in the valleys.

THE VALLEYS ARE BLESSED PLACES

Not very much grows on the mountaintops. Instead, things grow in the valleys. It is in the valley that we find life. Too often we miss God's blessing because we stay on the mountain when the will of the Father is that we descend into the valley. We attempt to cling to the spiritual experiences, and as a result, the blessing becomes an idol. As I know from experience, too much input and not enough output does not result in growth, it results in getting fat. My worry is that too many "soaking in His presence" meetings can become a self-indulgence if there are not corresponding times of giving away that which we have received. This also happens because we misunderstand where God is found. We find Him as we feed the hungry, give the thirsty a drink, clothe the naked, visit the prisoners and welcome strangers. He is found in the mundane as well as the roller coaster, in the still small voice as well as the earthquake, wind and fire.

I used to hate the final day of Soul Survivor festivals because I knew that many of the attendees would be going back to difficult situations and would find it hard to make the adjustment from the mountaintop to the valley. Then I realized that the proof of the value of the festival lies in the other 51 weeks of the year. God prepares us for mission. Mission happens where people are. Not many people live on the tops of mountains.

We can have the same attitude toward Bible teaching as we do toward spiritual experiences. "Give us more meat" is the cry. I believe as passionately in the teaching of the Word as I do about the infilling of the Holy Spirit. When we know the truth, the truth sets us free. There is a sense in which you cannot read the Bible too much. But there is also a sense in which you can. Vineyard movement leader John Wimber used to say, "The meat is on the street."[1] That means that there has to come a time when we don't just read and memorize the Word but also do it. The Bible is for so much more than learning—it is for obeying. Jesus said His food was to do the will of the One who sent Him (see John 4:34). Our meat is to live the Kingdom life in the midst of a broken and hurt world. The first Christians were not known as the people of the doctrine or as the people of the experience; they were first known as the people of the way because of how they lived their lives and the fact that Jesus is the Way. You want more meat? Don't just listen to the word—obey it.

The valley is the place where we discover whether we have a spirituality that works only in the church or one that works in the world. The

valley is often a place where we find ourselves whether we like it or not. But it is also a place to which we sometimes must choose to go. As Christians there is a temptation to retreat from the real world where there are real problems and real dilemmas with real people into a spirituality that depends on conference- or event-hopping. Every day I have a choice. I can choose either to cooperate with God in the valleys where He has

The valleys are not pauses between mountains; they are where Christianity is lived out.

placed me or to give up and take the easy option of ending my days singing happy songs while the world goes to hell. In a world where so much is measured by its results, and success is the test of the usefulness of any activity, God calls us to invest in obscurity. He calls us to redefine success as obedience before results. To care for the dying, the broken, the marginalized and the outcast of our society may not bring the warm fuzzies, but it blesses God.

It is relatively easy to meet with God at a Christian festival. The mature, however, also learn how to find Him in the mundane. True spiritual growth is to discover the paradox that we receive more when we give than we do when we focus on receiving. It is more blessed to give than to receive.

One of the most liberating discoveries in my walk with God has been that the valleys are blessed places. They are not pauses between mountains; the valleys are where Christianity is lived out. God will not have it any other way. Don't waste your life waiting for the next conference or the next event. He wants to speak to you as you do the gardening. He wants to bless you through a conversation with your neighbor. He will meet you as you serve. You will find Him as you befriend the lonely. You will receive as you give. Then you will be truly blessed.

Note
1. "Naturally Supernatural II," *Bluewater Bay United Church.* http://www. pechurchnet.co.za/bwbuc/teach/bteach166.htm (accessed July 17, 2003).

INVESTING IN OBSCURITY

Colin had worked for Soul Survivor for about seven years, leading our discipleship training course and drumming in the worship band. He was about to leave us to train to be an Anglican vicar at Ridley Hall in Cambridge. As we were chatting about his time with us, I asked him if there was any constructive criticism or advice he wanted to give me about Soul Survivor. He said something that I did not expect and that has stayed with me ever since. He expressed his concern that everything we were involved in had become quite public. "What do we do that is hidden?" he asked. Then came the question, "Where are we investing in obscurity?"

How much of what we do is in private, for the Lord's eyes only? Obviously our prayer and fasting should be in secret, without boasting; Jesus makes that very clear. But what about good deeds, works of service, acts of mercy and costly giving? As I thought about this, I felt more and more challenged. How much of what I do in my Christian life is for other people's consumption and how much is simply for

Christ? How much of my activity is directed at building a ministry and is therefore strategic and focused, and how much am I performing random acts of kindness that will never be known, do not have any payoff and are simply expressions of devotion to the Father? In a culture that worships success and values results, we are called to value people and express our worship in service of them.

WASTE YOUR TIME

When I began my job as youth pastor at Saint Andrew's, Chorleywood, I quickly found lots to do and became very busy. If I'm honest, I also felt more than a little important and took my role, and indeed myself, very seriously. One Sunday, before the morning service, I was rushing around being very important. I passed an elderly lady in our church named Hilda. She was sitting on one of the side pews, her walker parked next to her. As I passed she called out and motioned to me to sit next to her. I inwardly groaned as I thought of all the important things I still had to do. I sat down and said, "Hilda, this will have to be quick—I have a lot to do." She looked at me and said, "Mike, don't you just love Jesus? Isn't He wonderful? If ever you are passing by my house, just pop in—the back door is always open. We could worship and pray to Jesus together." Then as I got up to go, she gave my hand a squeeze and said, "I pray for you and the young people every day, you know." That conversation has stayed with me ever since. Hardly anyone has heard of Hilda. She has never been on TV, never played in a band, never, as far as I know, preached a sermon. I have a sneaking suspicion that she is pretty famous in heaven, though. She spent so much time with Jesus that there was a fragrance about her. I suddenly saw all my self-important busyness for what it was—filthy rags. Hilda had chosen the better thing. Hilda "wasted" herself on God; she gave of herself extravagantly. Mother Teresa of Calcutta spent her life serving the destitute and dying despite, or maybe even because of, the fact that they would never be in a position to give anything back. To give extravagantly is to give wastefully; to waste our time, money and talents on those who could never repay.

Hilda wasted herself on God; Mother Teresa on others. They were doing the same thing. To waste ourselves on others is to waste ourselves on God. To give to others is to worship God. Mother Teresa was once asked why she devoted herself to feeding the poor and caring for the dying. Her answer was simple and profound: for Jesus. "But love your enemies, do good to them, and lend to them without expecting to get anything back" (Luke 6:35).

Learning again to serve someone, and then to keep my mouth shut about it, is good for the soul.

There is something in us that craves attention. Our culture magnifies this tendency. We expect private lives to be public property. Every secret can be revealed for the right price, as we see with all the tabloid exclusives telling us about which famous people are having affairs with other famous people. The need to impress is part of human nature. For that reason, investing in obscurity should be added to the list of spiritual disciplines, alongside prayer, Bible study, confession, etc. Learning again to serve and give and help someone, and then to keep my mouth shut about it, is good for the soul. Don't even use your charitable act as an illustration in your small group. Sometimes people don't need to follow me as I follow Christ. Now and again they can just follow Christ.

CELEBRATE LIFE

A few days before writing this, I returned from a worship conference in Nashville, Tennessee. At the conference the worship leaders, musicians and speakers all congregated in the "green room" between meetings. Some of the time they discussed new albums, tours and other worship leaders and speakers. We all stayed in a very nice hotel. I arrived back in England in time to attend our "newcomers meal" for those who had joined our church in the last few months. I sat at a table with three guys who had been homeless and were currently staying in a shelter where some members of our church were volunteering. They did not seem very interested in record deals. They just wanted to talk about the hostel, their lives and Jesus. They were so real. They had no pretensions. They took me at face value. One of them asked if I was new to the church as well! To be honest, it frightened me. I came back from Nashville excited about the work of the Lord; they were more interested in the Lord of the work. Something else also struck me. They seemed genuinely interested in people. Their eyes didn't glaze over when they were listening to someone else speak. They were not glancing at their watches to see when the next appointment was. They were enjoying the moment.

Those who learn to invest in obscurity also seem to be the best at celebrating life. They are not so perpetually driven to achieve that they never take time to savor the moment. God instituted a series of festivals in Israel's year so that they would have occasions to celebrate. They even had celebrations in the desert, before they entered the Promised Land. I believe that God calls us to party on the journey and not wait until we reach the destination. To party is to celebrate life. To party when there is still work to do is to express trust that God is the creator and sustainer of all things, and therefore, we should not take ourselves too seriously.

Investing in obscurity is a spiritual discipline that joyfully celebrates the value of small things, the importance of the seemingly insignificant. More than that, it is to declare that God is found in the small things, He is discovered in the hidden places.

The Lord uses the desert times to reorder our priorities so that people become more important than tasks.

The visit of the Magi on the first Christmas illustrates this perfectly. When these foreigners arrived in Jerusalem and asked King Herod where the King of the Jews was to be born, the answer was surprising. He was not to be found in the capital or in a palace but in a little town called Bethlehem and in a stable. His birth was so obscure that the chief priests and teachers of the Law missed it. The only people who celebrated the birth of the Messiah were a group of foreign astrologers and some shepherds working the night shift. The important people were too busy doing important things.

One of the lessons of the desert is to learn to value the truly good things in life: friendships, the beauty of creation, the uniqueness of every person. The Lord uses the desert times to reorder our priorities so that people become more important than tasks. It is interesting to see how many times the gospel writers mention the fellowship meals Jesus had. Many of these meals were celebrations with His friends and also with the outcasts of society. Jesus was not too busy to spot Zacchaeus up a tree or to notice the woman with the issue of blood touching Him. He waited by Jacob's well to have a conversation with one Samaritan woman instead of marching into the town of Sychar to conduct an evangelistic crusade.

I fear that I may have missed many divine appointments because I have been too busy with my own agenda to notice God at work in the small things, to hear His still small voice whispering from the hidden places. "Who despises the day of small things?" asks the Lord in Zechariah 4:10. The answer: We do. Let us turn from our infatuation with numbers, wealth and power. Let us follow the God who came as a baby to an obscure little town, who chose a group of outcasts and failures to be His disciples and who was more interested in one sick woman who touched the hem of His garment than in a whole crowd. Jesus invested in obscurity. He has invested in you and me. May we find Him in the hidden places.

CHAPTER 8

LIFE IS TOUGH, BUT GOD IS GOOD

I used to think that once you became a Christian your problems would disappear, God would grant you anything you wanted and you would live a life of health, wealth and happiness. That was until I became a Christian. I used to think that people who stood on platforms at Christian meetings had things figured out, did not have any doubts and never felt low, lonely or out of their depth. That was until I stood on a platform. As soon as I became a Christian, I started to read biographies of famous charismatic Christian leaders. As I read these books, there seemed to be a miracle on every page. This should have encouraged me, but instead I was left feeling the opposite. The truth is that in my life there was not even a miracle in every chapter, let alone a miracle on every page. I felt like a spiritual failure, defeated and disqualified from God's service.

In the last few years, I have had the shock of my life as I have found myself standing on platforms, running festivals, leading a church and even writing books. Sometimes I still feel low, life can be a struggle, and all my issues are not resolved. To be perfectly honest, sometimes life is confusing and hurts like hell. For a while I was convinced that what I was doing was an accident and that when God discovered the true character of this broken human being doing these things, I would be out on my ear. Back to accounting for me.

Then two things happened. First, I met a friend who was a leader in the church and whom God was clearly using very powerfully. The previous few years of his life had been a bit of a nightmare. His wife was suffering from a serious illness, and she had been in and out of the hospital for two years. On one occasion he thought she might die. They had two little children at the time. As we talked he said something that shocked me and then comforted me: He said, "I have realized two things during this time. First, life's a bitch. Second, God is good." He said he had to face the reality that for him life was very hard. Even in God's presence his problems refused to disappear. Yet he had come to the place where he could say with integrity that God is good. He had met God in the pain and known His comfort and peace and, yes, even joy in the

This is the glory of the gospel, not that God takes us out of the world, but that He gives us His strength to walk through the pain of this world.

midst of the turmoil. This is the glory of the gospel, not that God takes us out of the world, but that He gives us His strength to walk through the pain and the suffering that are a necessary part of being human.

The second thing that happened was that I read Paul's first and second letters to the Corinthians with new eyes. I have always regarded Paul as the hard man of the Early Church. You did not mess with Paul. He planted more churches than anyone else, pioneered the taking of the gospel to the Gentiles and wrote most of the letters in the New Testament. However you measure success, it would be difficult to find a more successful Christian than the apostle Paul. If there was anyone who knew how to give the devil (and anyone else for that matter) a good kick in the teeth, it would be Paul. If there was anyone who could teach us a thing or two about victorious Christian living, it would be this superapostle. That is why his two letters to the church in Corinth are so shocking. The major theme of these two letters is not as I had supposed—the gifts of the Spirit or sexual morality or divisions in the Church. Instead, the major theme is finding God's strength in our weakness. Paul talks again and again about his sufferings, trials and vulnerabilities.

MEET GOD IN THE PAIN

I ask those of you who have been brought up on a gospel of health, wealth and prosperity to read the following passages carefully and with an open mind. "For I resolved to know nothing while I was with you except Jesus Christ and him crucified. I came to you in weakness and fear, and with much trembling" (1 Cor. 2:2-3). Paul went to the Corinthians in fear! He went with much trembling! He did not arrogantly march into town claiming the victory; he went in weakness.

To this very hour we go hungry and thirsty, we are in rags, we are brutally treated, we are homeless. We work hard with our own hands. When we are cursed, we bless; when we are persecuted, we endure it; when we are slandered, we answer kindly. Up to this moment we have become the scum of the earth, the refuse of the world (1 Cor. 4:11-13).

But we have this treasure in jars of clay to show that this all-surpassing power is from God and not from us. We are hard pressed on every side, but not crushed; perplexed, but not in despair; persecuted, but not abandoned; struck down, but not destroyed (2 Cor. 4:7-9).

I love the phrase "perplexed, but not in despair" because that is how I seem to spend a lot of my life: confused but not hopeless.

Rather, as servants of God we commend ourselves in every way: in great endurance; in troubles, hardships and distresses; in beatings, imprisonments and riots; in hard work, sleepless nights and hunger; in purity, understanding, patience and kindness; in the Holy Spirit and in sincere love; in truthful speech and in the power of God; with weapons of righteousness in the right hand and in the left; through glory and dishonor, bad report and good report; genuine, yet regarded as impostors; known, yet regarded as unknown; dying, and yet we live on; beaten, and yet not killed; sorrowful, yet always rejoicing; poor, yet making many rich; having nothing, and yet possessing everything (2 Cor. 6:4-10).

This passage is, I believe, one of the most glorious in all of Scripture. The phrase, "sorrowful, yet always rejoicing" deserves a book of its own. It captures the true balance of the Christian life. This is authentic Christian living. This is the antidote to a faith that owes more to Western consumerism than to the Word of God. It is out of suffering and death that life comes. If we have not learned this from the cross of Jesus, what have we learned? That is why Jesus Himself says, "If anyone would come after me, he must deny himself and take up his cross and follow me" (Mark 8:34). This is the true gospel that will change the world, not some shallow version typified by God finding us parking spaces instantly on a rainy day. Instead of asking for an instant parking space, how about asking for the Lord to grow in you the fruit of patience so that others might see more of Christ's likeness in you? Think about it: Will people flock to a God who provides parking spaces or to a God who demonstratively changes lives?

A friend of mine was watching Christian TV in the United States recently and she saw someone standing next to a wonderful Rolls Royce. The man was exhorting viewers to believe that God would make them rich. He said, "My Daddy in heaven loves me so much that He gave me this Rolls Royce." My friend found herself shouting at the TV, "No! My Daddy in heaven loves me so much that He gave me Jesus!"

Do you really want the highlight of your testimony to be that God gave you a car, or, like Abraham, do you want God Himself to be your shield and very great reward? I am not saying that God wants us to be poor. I am not saying that He does not look after His children or sometimes provide them with cars. He has done that for me (although not a Rolls!). The question is, What are we living for? What is it that excites us more than anything? Where is our treasure? There we will also find our heart.

In the following passage, Paul is attempting to answer those who are claiming that others are more qualified to be apostles than he is. He lists his qualifications for apostleship; and while he begins as you would expect, he then goes on to list certain things that one would think wouldn't qualify him as anything other than a failure.

> Are they Hebrews? So am I. Are they Israelites? So am I. Are they Abraham's descendants? So am I. Are they servants of Christ? (I am out of my mind to talk like this.) I am more. I have worked much harder, been in prison more frequently, been flogged more severely, and been exposed to death again and again. Five times I received from the Jews the forty lashes minus one. Three times I was beaten with rods, once I was stoned, three times I was shipwrecked, I spent a night and a day in the open sea, I have been constantly on the move. I have been in danger from rivers, in danger from bandits, in danger from my own countrymen, in danger from Gentiles; in danger in the city, in danger in the country, in danger at sea; and in danger from false brothers. I have labored and toiled and have often gone without sleep; I have known hunger and thirst and have often gone without food; I have been cold and naked. Besides everything else, I face daily the pressure of my concern for all the churches. Who is weak, and I do not feel weak? Who is led into sin, and I do not inwardly burn? (2 Cor. 11:22-29)

A couple of points here. First, how does anyone manage to get shipwrecked three times? You would have thought that after being shipwrecked twice Paul would have found himself alternative transport! Second, these passages do not simply speak of external pressure, but they also speak of inner turmoil. Yet Paul was more successful than any of us. The secret is not in having no hardships; the secret is persevering through hardships. That is why the gospel of "come to Jesus and life will be pain free" is no gospel at all. Following that message results in the sort of shallow believers Jesus described in the parable of the sower:

> The one who received the seed that fell on rocky places is the man who hears the word and at once receives it with joy. But since he has no root, he lasts only a short time. When trouble or persecution comes because of the word, he quickly falls away (Matt. 13:20-21).

William Carey is regarded as one of the founders of the modern missionary movement. In the eighteenth century he went to India and was the first of many missionaries to that nation. He translated the Scriptures into several local dialects and founded a society that would later send missionaries all over the world. But William Carrey's history would never have suggested he would accomplish so much. Listen to this description of his background given by Robert J. Morgan:

> William Carey was born in 1761 in a forgotten village (Paulerspury in Northamptonshire) in the dullest period of the dullest of all centuries. His family was poor and he was poorly educated. A skin affliction made him sensitive to out-door work, so he apprenticed to a nearby shoemaker. When he didn't do well at cobbling, he opened a school to supplement his income. That didn't go well either. He married, but his marriage proved unhappy. A terrible disease took the life of his baby daughter and left Carey bald for life. He was called to

pastor a small church, but he had trouble being ordained because of his boring sermons.[1]

This man became one of the founders of the modern missionary movement and a hero of the faith! At the end of his life, he knew that people would try to write his biography, so he wrote to his son-in-law these words:

> Eustace, if after my removal any one should think it worth his while to write my life, I will give you a criterion by which you may judge its correctness. If he gives me credit for being a plodder he will describe me justly. Anything beyond this will be too much. I can plod. I can persevere in any definite pursuit. To this I owe everything.[2]

William learned to plod because of all the setbacks in his life. He may not have been the most able person God could have chosen, but he was the most available. Those of us who know ourselves to be weak and broken have a choice to make. We can wallow in our weakness and write ourselves off because of our brokenness, or we can look to the God who delights in using the weak things of this world to shame the strong, and the foolish things of this world to shame the wise.

Live as Real People

The problem with the theology of the permanent smile—pretending to have a life without pain—is that it produces Christians who live dual lives. Their church life is full of empty Christian clichés and platitudes. Then there is the secret, guilt-ridden life filled with doubts, failures and even depression. Of course, the Lord wants to deal with our doubts, release us from our failures and heal our depression. He cannot and will not do that, however, if we do not acknowledge that these problems exist. In recent years many of us have learned how to laugh in church, and that has been liberating. Now we need to learn how to cry. Someone said, "If you can't bleed in a hospital, where can you bleed? If you can't cry in a church, where can you cry?" Church should be where the real people are, not plastic people with plastic faces. I am wary of trusting any leader who does not walk with a limp. Perfect leaders with no problems are too good to be true.

If the Lord took away all obstacles, problems and pain, He would be making life easier for us than He did for the first disciples.

If the Lord took away all our obstacles, problems and pain, He would be making life easier for us than He did for the first disciples. Indeed, He would be making life easier for us than for His own Son. Why on earth would He want to do that? As He did with William Carey and the apostle Paul, God will use us in our weakness. Let us stop pretending and say with Paul:

> Therefore I will boast all the more gladly about my weaknesses, so that Christ's power may rest on me. That is why, for

Christ's sake, I delight in weaknesses, in insults, in hardships, in persecutions, in difficulties. For when I am weak, then I am strong (2 Cor. 12:9-10).

Notes
1. Robert J. Morgan, quoted in Ross Paterson, *The Antioch Factor* (Kent, England: Sovereign World Ltd., 2001), n.p.
2. William Carey, quoted in Ross Paterson, *The Antioch Factor* (Kent, England: Sovereign World Ltd., 2001), n.p.

CHAPTER 9

THE DESERT OF OBEDIENCE

There are times when we find ourselves in the desert because we have made wrong choices or we have been disobedient. But there are also times when we find ourselves in the desert not because we have done anything wrong but simply because it is the place where God can attract our undivided attention. This is the type of desert that is the major subject of this book. There is a third type of desert experience, however, and that is the desert of obedience. There is a cost to living a life of obedience, and Jesus told us that we should count the cost of following Him before we set out on the journey. Obedience to the will of God means that we deny ourselves and take up our cross in order to follow Him (see Mark 8:34). Obedience to the will of the Father was costly for Jesus. His agony in the garden of Gethsemane was an agony of obedience. He said to the disciples, "My soul is overwhelmed with sorrow to the point of death" (Matt. 26:38). He was then overheard praying, "My Father, if it is possible, may this cup be taken from me. Yet not as I will, but as you will" (Matt. 26:39). Jesus' choice to go to the cross was a choice to go through "the valley of the shadow of death" (Ps. 23:4). Three years earlier he was "led by the Spirit in the desert" (Luke 4:1). He chose to follow the Holy Spirit's lead. He went to the desert when it would have been more comfortable to stay in Nazareth.

THE COST OF OBEDIENCE

As a follower of Christ there will be many times when I will have to choose between the will of my Father and my own will. Frank Sinatra sang "I did it my way." But the song of the Christian has to be "I did

it His way." This is a crucial principle in an age where we are told that we have a right to happiness and fulfillment and that life must be a pursuit of these things. Jesus taught that happiness is a by-product of obedience. "Blessed [happy] are those who hunger and thirst for righteousness, for they will be filled" (Matt. 5:6).

Jesus taught that happiness is a by-product of obedience.

For obedience to be obedience it has to be specific. It is about the decisions we make. It is about seeking to find His will for our lives and then embracing it. We discover His will supremely in the Bible and choose to follow it:

- I will not have sex outside marriage.
- I will use every opportunity to tell others about Jesus.

- I will be generous with my possessions, time and talents.
- I will respond kindly to those who are rude to me.
- I will make it a priority to pray and read my Bible.

The above choices are not ones where we wait for prophetic words before we implement them. God spoke about these issues and many others in the Bible and He has not changed His mind since then. There are other choices we make that require us to listen to His voice with a heart that is willing to respond:

- Do I take this job or promotion?
- Do I marry this person?
- Is God calling me to be a Christian rock star or an accountant? (This may seem strange, but occasionally God calls some to be accountants!)

These questions require us to seek out the Lord. What are the general principles we find in the Bible? What do Christian friends discern? Is God speaking through circumstances? What does common sense tell us? Has God spoken through the gift of prophecy to confirm the leading of other discernments? The point of this is that sometimes God's will and ours will not coincide. At these times are we willing not only to hear but also to obey the Lord?

Sometimes the desert of obedience is a desert of misunderstanding. Those close to us will disagree with or be offended by a decision we have made. Perhaps those not so close to us will question our motives. This is where the rubber meets the road. Do we live to please other people or God?

Sometimes the desert of obedience is a desert of unfulfilled dreams. I know people who were desperately in love, yet God told them not to marry—and they obeyed, even though for a while it broke their hearts. Sometimes the desert of obedience is a desert of broken relationships.

Blessed are you when people insult you, persecute you and falsely say all kinds of evil against you because of me. Rejoice and be glad, because great is your reward in heaven, for in the same way they persecuted the prophets who were before you (Matt. 5:11-12).

THE JOY OF OBEDIENCE

It is one of the mysteries of the faith that one can experience joy in the midst of tears, peace in the middle of the storm.

Why did Jesus live a life and die a death of obedience? The writer to the Hebrews provides the answer: "Let us fix our eyes on Jesus, the author and perfecter of our faith, who for the joy set before him endured the cross, scorning its shame, and sat down at the right hand of the throne of God" (Heb. 12:2). The motivation for obedience is joy!

There is a prize at the end of the road of obedience and that is sharing the joy of our Father and of His Son, Jesus Christ.

The reward is heaven, and the prize is eternity with Jesus! We receive the prize when we die, but it is also available here and now. It is difficult to describe the joy of obedience. Paul had a stab at it when he described himself as "sorrowful, yet always rejoicing" (2 Cor. 6:10). There is a unique intimacy with God that comes when you find yourself in the desert of obedience. It is one of the mysteries of the faith that one can experience joy in the midst of tears, peace in the middle of the storm.

THE CHOICE TO OBEY

When I was the youth pastor at Saint Andrew's Anglican Church in Chorleywood, I loved the job and I loved the young people. They were my extended family. I have memories of those days that are so precious: the kids who became Christians, the outings and house parties, the meetings when God flooded the room with His tangible presence, the one-on-one conversations.

Then one day the Lord spoke to me and told me I was to resign as the youth leader. I desperately did not want to. Why would the Lord say that? It did not make sense. *I must have heard wrong*, I thought. But the impression would not leave me. I could not escape His voice. Eventually I told the vicar, David Pytches, that I felt it was time for me to give up being the youth leader. He graciously gave me another job, working with adults. I struggled. I missed the young people desperately. I could not understand what was going on. It felt like I was in the wilderness. Working with grown-ups was so boring! Everything happened in slow motion. I began to wonder if I had made the wrong decision, but there was no going back. Sometimes it was agony. Then after two years, we began Soul Survivor, the youth ministry where I now serve. Looking back, it could not have happened if I had not given up the youth work. There would never have been the space. I was given a choice. I could either obey the prompting of the Spirit even though I did not understand it at the time, or I could play it safe. I wonder what would have happened—or rather, not have happened—if I had played it safe.

Over the years I have met some very gifted people who, for some reason or another, have never quite fulfilled their potential. Then there are others who may not be any more talented or gifted, but for whom it seems true that everything they touch turns to gold. This seems to happen as much in the spiritual realm as it does in secular society. I have wondered why this is so. I think there are probably many reasons. One has to be the mystery of God's sovereign choice. Why was Abraham chosen out of all the wandering nomads of Haran at the time? Why Israel out of all the Middle Eastern tribes? Why those 12 to be disciples? Why Saul on the road to Damascus and not the guy riding next to him? Why David and not one of his brothers? Why Moses and not Aaron? There is an element of mystery to God's sovereignty that we would do well to bow toward rather than attempt to dissect and put in an intellectual box.

We have to acknowledge that there is a strong element of His choice in these things, but I suggest that another element is our choices. Those whom God plans to use He gives opportunities to make good choices, often early in their Christian lives. Conversely, I have met some gifted people over the years who seem constantly to make bad life choices and as a result seem to be forever walking around the mountain rather than climbing up it. They either cannot see their area of gifting and constantly strive for a ministry and recognition in other things, or they always seem to be in the wrong place at the wrong time with the wrong people. It can be incredibly frustrating to watch.

Someone to whom God has given a good deal of favor over the years is my friend Matt Redman. Some would say it is because he is a gifted worship leader and songwriter. It is because of God's sovereign choice. There are other gifted worship leaders and songwriters who have not been given the same profile as Matt. Partly, however, I am convinced that he has been given favor because of the choices he made as a young boy. From age 13 Matt loved drama, and I used to go and watch him playing the lead role in school plays. He was in a school that had a great reputation for drama, and he received a good deal of recognition from his teachers and peers alike. Then when he was about 16, Matt was invited to be the first student in the history of Watford Boys Grammar School to produce and direct the school play. He did a great job and his standing at the school increased.

One day Matt came to see me and said that the Lord had told him to give up drama so that he could concentrate on improving his music, since his calling was to be a worship leader and not an actor. I was confused and concerned. I knew how much the acting meant to Matt, and I tried to persuade him that maybe he had misheard the Lord—surely he could do both. Matt wouldn't listen to me; he had made up his mind. The immediate result was that he went through a nightmare at school as neither his teachers nor his fellow students could understand his decision. He also had to go through the pain of seeing his friends take part in future productions without him.

In hindsight it may seem like an obviously right decision. The point, however, is that at the time Matt had hardly led worship outside our youth group, let alone written a song that anyone else could sing! Matt was faithful in what now appears a small thing, and the Lord has given him the opportunity to be faithful in big things. I think that is how it works. It is all about choices. Obedience is a choice we make every day. We can do nothing about the Lord's choices, but we can do everything about ours.

CHAPTER 10

JOSEPH—LIFE'S NOT FAIR!

The story of Joseph is one of the great tales of the Bible. It has so much to teach us on so many levels that whole books have been written about it. However, I want to confine myself to looking at one aspect of Joseph's life, and that is how his wilderness years prepared him for the eventual fulfillment of his dreams. Joseph's story begins in Genesis 37:

> Joseph, a young man of seventeen, was tending the flocks with his brothers, the sons of Bilhah and the sons of Zilpah, his father's wives, and he brought their father a bad report about them.
>
> Now Israel [Jacob] loved Joseph more than any of his other sons, because he had been born to him in his old age; and he made a richly ornamented robe for him. When his brothers saw that their father loved him more than any of

them, they hated him and could not speak a kind word to him
(vv. 2-4).

Joseph was the favorite—there was no question about it. He was born
to Jacob in his old age and he was also the son of Rachel, the wife Jacob
loved the most. There may have been other reasons. There may have
been no reasons. It is unfair as well as irrational for a father to love one
of his children more than the others. It is not just unfair to the other
kids, but it is also unfair and destructive for the favorite who often goes
through life with a touch of arrogance and a sense of superiority that
brings many enemies. Many times these favorite children suffer for
their arrogance. It is very difficult to love those who seem to have an
exaggerated ability to love themselves. When you are the favorite everyone knows it. Joseph knew. While all the brothers were out working in
the fields Joseph was at home "resting" with his dad. As if this were not
bad enough, Joseph was a snitch: "He brought their father a bad report
about them" (v. 2). Isn't this just like the youngest in the family? Then
to top it off, Joe gets the coat of many colors! That would be the equiv-
alent of the youngest getting a car for his seventeenth birthday when
the others had to make do with bikes. No wonder the brothers were
upset. The final straw came when Joseph announced to his brothers
and his parents that he had had a couple of dreams and the message
was that his brothers and parents would one day bow before him. Even
Jacob, his father, was taken aback by this and rebuked him (see Gen.
37:5-11).

Now we all have dreams. Some dreams we never tell anyone about
because we would seem so arrogant. I have had a dream for many years
now that I play soccer for Manchester United in the Champions League
final, score the winning goal and appear on *Celebrity Big Brother* TV

show and win. I would then be knighted by the queen: Sir Michael of Watford! I would never tell anyone about this; they would just laugh at me. Sometimes a dream can seem a fantasy until it comes to pass.

This brings us to the other problem with Joseph's dreams—the big problem. The dreams were from God. Why Joseph? Why does God sometimes choose the wrong people? The failures. The ones with character deficiencies. Why does He not always go for the ones who are stable and dependable? Why did He choose me? Why did He choose you for that matter? I don't know. It is part of the mystery of God and I am happy to leave it there. He chose Joseph all right. Sure enough, one day Joseph's brothers and his parents would bow before him. But something had to happen first. Joe needed to be prepared for that moment. God chose an arrogant, sneaky, pampered 17-year-old and then took him into the wilderness so that when the bowing and the adulation came, they came to a different person. Some have suggested that Joseph had all the good character traits within him and that the wilderness time was simply the opportunity for them to come out. I don't agree. I think God *remade* Joseph in the desert.

So what happened to him? To cut an interesting story very short, his brothers sold him into slavery, and he ended up a slave in Egypt, far away from his family. How his dreams must have come back to haunt him. For a while things began to look up. A man named Potiphar bought him, and Joseph did so well that he was rapidly promoted and became the most trusted slave in the house. He was the slave with the highest status, but he was still a slave. Then it all went wrong again, and this time it was not his fault. Potiphar was out of town for some meetings and Mrs. Potiphar, who had clearly taken a liking to the slave, propositioned Joseph. "Come to bed with me" were, I think, her exact words (Gen. 39:12). Joseph declined the invitation—a response that rather upset Mrs. Potiphar—and so she accused him of rape. Mr. Potiphar naturally had to side with his wife over a mere slave, and Joseph found himself in prison. He was there for rather a long time. Eventually the baker and the cupbearer to Pharaoh were thrown into the same prison as Joseph. They both had strange dreams that Joseph interpreted. The cupbearer was released from prison and restored to his previous role, just as Joseph had prophesied. The interpretation of the baker's dream was not quite so encouraging. He was hanged. I love the way Joseph pleaded with the cupbearer after he had interpreted the dream:

> But when all goes well with you, remember me and show me kindness; mention me to Pharaoh and get me out of this prison. For I was forcibly carried off from the land of the Hebrews, and even here I have done nothing to deserve being put in a dungeon (Gen. 40:14-15).

What happens when the cupbearer is released is therefore quite painful: "The chief cupbearer, however, did not remember Joseph; he forgot him" (Gen. 40:23). How his brothers would have loved to see him now! "What goes around, comes around" is the phrase. If there were any time Joseph was close to despair, it would have been now. Yes, he was far from blameless when he was sold into slavery, but since then it seemed the more he tried to do things right, the more they went wrong. I wonder how close he came to giving up completely.

Then things suddenly began to change. Pharaoh had a couple of disturbing dreams that no one could interpret, the cupbearer remembered Joseph, and he was immediately released. Joseph interpreted the dreams and suddenly became prime minister of Egypt. What a turn-around! From prison to prime minister. Joseph worked hard during the seven years of good harvests; and then when the seven years of famine came, Egypt was the only country in the entire region that was able to cope. Joseph's family members were starving, and eventually, in desperation his brothers traveled to Egypt to beg. Not recognizing Joseph, they bowed down before him as they begged for food for their family.

This surely was the moment of revenge, the moment of vindication, but Joseph's response was not the anticipated one. After years of suffering because of the actions of his brothers, he responds very differently from the way he would have at the beginning of the story. He weeps for them. He embraces them. Why? Because this Joseph is different from the brash 17-year-old we saw at first. What changed Joseph? Years in the desert changed Joseph. How did he change?

REMADE IN THE DESERT

First, Joseph learned about God's sovereignty. Joseph hadn't taken a course of lectures in reformed theology at Bible college, but rather, He learned about God's sovereignty in the hard school of life. This is how he revealed himself to his brothers:

> Then Joseph said to his brothers, "Come close to me." When they had done so, he said, "I am your brother Joseph, the one you sold into Egypt! And now, do not be distressed and do not be angry with yourselves for selling me here, because it was to save lives that God sent me ahead of you. For two years now there has been famine in the land, and for the next five years there will not be ploughing and reaping. But God sent me

ahead of you to preserve for you a remnant on earth and to save your lives by a great deliverance."

"So then, it was not you who sent me here, but God" (Gen. 45:4-8).

What an amazing statement: "It was not you who sent me here, but God." The wilderness years teach us that when God wants to close

When God wants to close a door, no human being can open it; and when God chooses to open a door, no human being can close it.

a door, no human being can open it; and when God chooses to open a door, no human being can close it. In the desert we come to the end of ourselves, and therefore, we learn to trust the Almighty.

Throughout my 20s I longed to do the things I do now. I was desperate to preach, lead and pastor. But I was an accountant. I tried everything. I worked harder in church than anyone else. I practically lived in the building. The harder I pushed the doors, the more they seemed to stay closed. I was puzzled, as I genuinely believed that my dreams were from God and that there was a calling on my life that was not being fulfilled. It was agony. Then, just when I had virtually given up, at the age of 29 the doors opened— suddenly. I know who opened the doors. It was no human being. When things are tough now I look back and remember that He is sovereign, He is Lord. To know that I am not here because of my own efforts or gifts or manipulations is a deep comfort and abiding security. I now know that my 20s were not wasted years. On the contrary, they were the crucial years. With God there is no waste in the wasteland. The only waste is when we walk away.

Second, Joseph lost his arrogance and conceit. He greeted his brothers with tears of brokenness and tears of joy: "Do not be angry with yourselves." In the wilderness we come face-to-face with reality— the reality of who we are and the reality of who God is. It is a lesson we never forget. We know our fragility, our weakness and our sin, and we understand what grace is. In the wilderness we learn to lean on Him. Joseph was broken during his wilderness years but broken in a good and glorious way. He was broken so that the fragrance of God could flow throughout his life. He was broken so that the treasure would radiate through the jar of clay.

Joseph learned humility and service in the wilderness years. Eventually, when the family found themselves bowing down before Joseph, he knelt with them. He did not bask in the glory of the moment; he just wanted to serve.

God chose Joseph all right. He chose him to be a vessel through whom He would show His glory. The period between the dreams and their fulfillment is the most important and blessed time of all. It is the time of preparation so that when the dreams are fulfilled, we are not destroyed in the process.

Finally, in His sovereignty, God gave Joseph a choice. It is the choice we are all faced with. In the pain and isolation and unfairness of it all, Joseph had the choice either to turn from God and get bitter or to turn to God and get better. The choice is to say yes to God and

change or to stay ruler of our own lives. Only those who bow the knee in the desert of suffering will be able to stand the test in the season of prosperity.

The period between the dreams and their fulfilment is the most important and blessed time of all.

THE PURPOSE OF THE DESERT

So what is the goal of the desert? The goal is Jesus and the destination is heaven. The goal is to be changed more and more into the image of Jesus and to pursue Him until the day comes when we see Him face-to-face. Soul Survivor Watford, the church I pastor, is quite a young church. It is full of teenagers and young married couples. That means that we do a lot of matching (weddings) and hatching (babies), but so far not much dispatching (funerals)! I have told my church that I look forward to burying many of them in the years to come.

Having been involved in many weddings and having observed the preparations up close, I have occasionally wondered why people put themselves through the agony of it all. Months are taken up with preparations. Receptions are booked, flowers ordered, dresses made, in-laws negotiated and guests invited. The stress is sometimes enormous and things inevitably go wrong. Rarely do all the relevant parties agree on anything, and the whole thing costs a ridiculous amount of money. Then comes the big day. Whatever stresses arose the night before are forgotten, and the day is one of joy and celebration. The things that seemed so important in the buildup become somehow irrelevant. The relatives who spent the previous three months arguing are suddenly best friends as they pass the tissues to one another.

We are heading for the mother of all marriages, the wedding of all weddings. The preparations may sometimes be tough, the arrangements complicated and there may be disappointments on the way, but we are preparing for the marriage feast of the Lamb. Jesus, the Bridegroom, is preparing His Bride—and that Bride is you and me. This life is the preparation. We are being given our manicure. Is the preparation worth it? There can only be one answer for those who love the Bridegroom.

We have, so far, focused on the pain of the desert; now we will look at the ultimate purpose and goal so that we "do not lose heart" (Heb. 12:5). In order to face pain, we have to see purpose.

SPENDING ETERNITY WITH JESUS

I am currently going through the pain of a diet. For someone who adores food as much as I do, it is a nightmare. Why is it that all the meals that are tasty, delicious and satisfying are bad for you? Why do all the foods that are good for you have the texture of cardboard and the taste of nothing? Take celery, for example. I hate celery—with a passion. If one more person tells me that I burn more calories by eating celery than I derive from the celery, I may not be responsible for my actions. I have now spent three months munching celery sticks. I even put some through a vegetable juice extractor in the hope that they might taste better as a drink. They didn't. As if dieting were not bad enough, I am also exercising regularly at the gym. I haven't decided which is worse: the pain of doing the weights or the boredom of swimming. You may ask, Why do I do this to myself? Why do I put myself through it? It is because I see the goal, the prize. One day I will walk down the street and ladies will faint. They will take photos of me and want my autograph. David Beckham will be yesterday's man. Now some may question whether my goal is realistic, but it is the belief that there is a prize that keeps me going.

In Hebrews 12:2 we are told to "fix our eyes on Jesus, the author and perfecter of our faith, who for the joy set before him endured the cross, scorning its shame, and sat down at the right hand of the throne of God." What was

The trials of this life only assume real meaning when they are seen in the light of eternity.

Jesus' goal, His prize? The joy set before Him was to please His Father and as a result to bring transformation and salvation to the human race—to save us so that we would live with Him for eternity.

What is our goal, our prize? To spend eternity with Him! The incentive to keep on with the training (and the desert is the training) is to see Jesus. It is worth it because Jesus is worth it. The trials of this life only assume real meaning when they are seen in the light of eternity. Our heavenly Father uses the desert times not only to make us more useful in this world but also to create in us a hunger and a passion to meet Him in the next. The problem with the prosperity gospel is that it panders to our desire to be comfortable and satisfied in this life. When we have health, wealth and happiness without preparation in the desert, we become spiritually dull and we lose the plot.

One of the hardest things for God to do is to prosper you. Look at the history of Israel. Whenever the Israelites prospered, they turned away from God to idols. The Lord had to take them to the deserts of suffering and exile so that they would turn and follow Him again. I am not saying the Lord does not want to prosper us, but He has to train us in the desert first so that prosperity does not ruin us. God's plan is to bring us to the same place as the apostle Paul when he wrote to the Philippians:

For I have learned to be content whatever the circumstances. I know what it is to be in need, and I know what it is to have plenty. I have learned the secret of being content in any and every situation, whether well fed or hungry, whether living in plenty or in want. I can do everything through him who gives me strength (Phil. 4:11-13).

This is not our home—our citizenship is in heaven. Our home is our Father's house. Without a vision of heaven, we lose our cutting edge on Earth. For myself and my friends and colleagues at Soul Survivor, money and the lack thereof have been the desert that God has regularly used to keep our vision of eternity bright. God has blessed and used us more over the last 10 years than we could ever have dreamed or hoped. The temptation has sometimes been to believe the publicity and enjoy some of the sillier things one or two people have said to us.

Whenever pomposity and pride begin to rear their ugly heads and we are in danger of thinking that God is using us because we are special or anointed and not because He is merciful and gracious and loves to use the foolish things of the world to shame the wise, He always sends us a financial crisis. How I hate and love the financial crises. I hate them because they are painful and uncomfortable. I feel helpless and out of control. I feel like a little boy who needs his dad. I love them because God uses them to cause me to trust in His provision again. I once again choose to live a life of dependence.

The Lord has regularly performed miracles just when we needed them. It is very interesting to me that He has never performed a miracle before we needed it. Miracles are supernatural breakthroughs of heaven to Earth. I believe they happen to remind us of our destiny, to cause us to look up. They speak to us of eternity. A few hundred years ago the slaves in the American south would sing "spirituals"—songs of heaven. These were songs of hope in the desert of slavery. Today our Lord invites us once again to sing songs of hope in the desert, to discover a faith for the future in the valley of the present.

GROWING LIKE JESUS

In the desert God takes us deeper in order to take us further. We are prepared for the wedding feast of heaven, but we are also prepared for service on Earth. The most dangerous people in any church or ministry are the people who are all gifting and no heart. They eventually destroy more than they build. Human beings look at the outward appearance (looks, abilities, etc.), but God looks at the heart (see 1 Sam. 16:7). The desert is the training ground that prepares us for life and a ministry that is trustworthy. In the desert we grow in passion for God and His ways; humility is birthed in us and we develop a meekness that inquires of the Lord instead of rushing to make decisions out of our own wisdom. We learn to put first things first; our priorities are changed. We grow to love people above success. In summary, we are changed into His likeness (see 2 Cor. 3:18). Christ is formed in us—His mercy and tenderness, His compassion and joy. So many of God's people long for

transformation. The good news is that it's possible. We can be changed. There are, however, no shortcuts. As we sit in the desert and begin there to behold His glory, we become more like Him.

Don't be satisfied any longer to exist in security; choose to live in adventure.

Don't settle for a superficial version of Christianity. Superficial Christianity is the most boring thing in the world. Go for broke! Ask your Lord to take you deeper. Don't be satisfied any longer to exist in security; choose to live in adventure. Say yes to His plans for you, and as He begins to unfold them, stay there. Don't run away. Then you will come up from the desert, leaning on your lover, ready to be a voice and not another echo, equipped to change the world.

More Breakthrough Books
from Soul Survivor

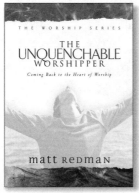

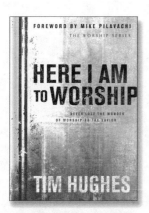

A RADICALLY NEW WAY TO REACH YOUNG PEOPLE

soul survivor encounter

If you want to inspire and equip young people, **Soul Survivor Encounter** is the key. Originating in England, Soul Survivor has released young leaders for Christ by teaching them about worship, action evangelism and social justice.

With **Soul Survivor Encounter**, you can use the successful elements of the Soul Survivor ministry to create in your young people a passionate commitment to worshiping God and putting their faith into action.

This biblical and relevant program is sure to ignite a revolution in youth ministry that will impact generations to come. Be a part of it!

Soul Survivor Kit
5 *Real Life & Living Out Loud Student Magazines*, 1 *Real Life & Living Out Loud Leader's Guide*, 1 *Real Life & Living Out Loud DVD*, *Soul Survivor Guide to Youth Ministry*, *Soul Survivor Prayer Ministry*, and *Soul Survivor Guide to Service Projects*.
ISBN 08307.35267

Real Life & Living Out Loud Student Magazine
ISBN 08307.35364

Real Life & Living Out Loud Leader's Guide
ISBN 08307.35313

Real Life & Living Out Loud DVD
UPC 607135.008927

Soul Survivor Guide to Youth Ministry
ISBN 08307.35305

Soul Survivor Prayer Ministry
ISBN 08307.35275

Soul Survivor Guide to Service Projects
ISBN 08307.35291

Soul Survivor Encounter is available at your local Christian bookstore or by calling 1-800-4-GOSPEL.

www.SoulSurvivorEncounter.com

Gospel Light